D1616210

1920s FASHION

Published in 2021 by Welbeck

An imprint of the Welbeck Non-Fiction Limited, part of Welbeck Publishing Group,
20 Mortimer Street, London W1T 3JW

First published in 2011 by Fiell Publishing Limited and in 2015 by Goodman Fiell

Text copyright © Charlotte Fiell and Emmanuelle Dirix 2021

All rights reserved. No part of this publication may be reproduced, stored in
a retrieval system, or transmitted in any form or by any means, electronically,
mechanical, photocopying, recording or otherwise, without the prior permission of
the copyright owners and the publishers.

A catalogue record for this book is available from the
British Library

Editorial: Katie Meegan
Design: Katie Baxendale
Picture sourcing: Charlotte Fiell & Clementine Fiell
Production: Marion Storz
Preface text: Charlotte Fiell
Introductory text: Emmanuelle Dirix
Captions & Biographies: Emmanuelle Dirix & Charlotte Fiell
Cover Illustration: Francesca Waddell/Lipstick of London Ltd

Printed in Dubai
ISBN 978-1-78739-887-0

1920s FASHION

THE DEFINITIVE SOURCEBOOK

Charlotte Fiell
Introduction by Emmanuelle Dirix

WELBECK

La femme chic

SUPPLÉMENT - Nº 190. Pl. 154.

ENSEMBLE CONFORTABLE POUR LES JOURS FROIDS
ÉXÉCUTÉ AVEC LES " PIQUES ZIBLIKASHA "

Preface

The 1920s were a period of unbridled optimism with people looking to the future and putting their trust in technological progress. The First World War had changed the very fabric of society and in its wake had brought women unprecedented freedoms and, of course, this was reflected in the fashions they chose to wear. From silk sack dresses and T-bar shoes to tight-fitting cloche hats and elegantly casual sportswear, the fashionable flappers and 'bright young things' of this era sought youthful clothes that were in accord with their more liberated lives, and in so doing helped to democratize fashion for the first time in its history.

This unique publication seeks to explore this phenomenon by showcasing over 500 original photographs and skilfully drawn illustrations that reveal an extraordinary diversity of styles that were offered by not only the well-known Parisian haute couture houses but also by department stores and mail-order catalogues. In addition, the introductory essay seeks to contextualise and explains the driving socio-economic and political forces of this period in relation to its fashions. It is hoped, therefore, that this publication will not only allow the rediscovery of many fashion designers and fashion illustrators, whose undeniable talents have until now been lost in the mists of time, but that it will also help bring a wider understanding of Art Deco fashion.

By comprehensively documenting the elegant silhouettes, exquisite detailing and masterful tailoring of 1920s fashions, this book should prove to be an invaluable source of information for fashion historians, whilst also providing a rich font of inspiration for fashion designers, vintage collectors and, of course, all self-respecting fashionistas.

Left
'Comfortable' dress and coat ensemble for 'cold days' with 'Piques ZibliKasha' motifs. *La Femme Chic*, 1926

Contents

Twenties Fashion

Fashionable Timing

This sourcebook looks in detail at fashion in a single decade, between the years 1920 and 1929. It's a common historical technique to parcel time up into the ten-year periods that fall between years ending with a nought, naming the decades (the 1920s, 1930s, 1940s and so on) accordingly. It is as if the passing of time can be organised into unique and distinctive eras. Unfortunately, the reality is somewhat different – the events that form both our culture and history don't always follow the calendar: things happen, often before or after a decade begins. In fashion terms, the Twenties is no exception to this, and many of the ideas, developments and designs we associate with that period of time actually took root much earlier. The story of fashion in the 1920s starts, in fact, a good few years before the decade began.

This is not to say that the 1920s did not offer anything new; indeed quite the contrary, and each page of this book tells a story of the new and the modern. But the novelty and modernity of the looks presented here needs to be seen in a much wider context if we are to understand quite how radical and exciting these fashions were for women.

This should come as no surprise; common sense alone tells us that fashion is rarely revolutionary in the way that the fashion press and popular histories would have us believe. In the same way that rarely one designer is responsible for changing the entire look of a woman's wardrobe, so no one simple set of dates can be stuck on such a process either.

Thus for example the straighter silhouettes that would later become the boyish shapes we associate with flappers had been introduced as early as 1907; the bright colours and exoticism so synonymous with 1920s evening wear, had equally been introduced into high fashion via various other broader cultural influences, as well as through the work of progressive fashion designers in previous decades. But it would take the 1920s to synthesise all these elements in the jubilant post-war zeitgeist, which provided such a fertile breeding ground for the magnificent and varied fashions we associate with the age.

In this way, it's not the fact that many of the characteristics of 1920s fashion make their debut in earlier years that is important, but the fact that they all come together in that period. The Twenties was a time of significant social and cultural shifts, and as such is an exciting and unique era to study through the lens of fashion.

The story of fashion is never just a story of fashion. Fashion is part of culture, and it's not created in an ivory tower. It is a visual language, full of clues we can read about the morals and values of the society that produced it. By examining fashion, we can study the very fabric of society, and this book allows for exactly such a study. A rich collection of fashion images from the 1920s is contained within these pages, including some photographs but predominantly fashion illustration (photography had yet to supersede illustration – colour stocks had still to be invented, and it was impossible to capture fine detailing on film). However, this is not a limitation, indeed quite the opposite; for the style of illustration and imaginary backdrops that were used to show off the garments all contribute to a much wider picture. Indeed, because the illustrations are taken from such a broad spectrum of publications – from the high-end, hand-tinted Parisian *Gazette du Bon Ton* featuring the most luxurious offerings from the haute couturiers, to the ready-to-wear fashions in the Printemps department store catalogue – it paints a realistic picture of what women from different echelons of society wore and allows us to make a visual comparison of how elite fashions came to influence cheaper ready-made garments.

Opposite
Silent film starlet Sally O'Neil
wear a lamé cloche hat and strings
of pearls, c.1925

Left
A mauve crêpe Georgette evening dress
embroidered with large silver pearls,
draped at the side held by ribbons in
different shades. *Dernières Creations*,
c.1923

The Flapper & 1920s Style

No other decade is quite so alive and vivid in popular consciousness as the 1920s; Art Deco, the Jazz Age, *les années folles*, the Roaring Twenties. Numerous films, TV shows, exhibitions and books have been dedicated to the era and the various movements within it, and fashion plays a pivotal role in all of these. It would be impossible to picture the Twenties without imagining young flappers in beaded dresses, with short hair and boyish silhouettes dancing the night away. Puffing on cigarettes and flashing their knees as they danced, their genteel, Edwardian mothers would have been appalled.

However, this new female brazenness is only part of a larger, more complex and more varied picture of women, their fashions and their bodies. So to focus only on the flapper would be to miss, and misinterpret, so many other important developments at the time. The emphasis placed on the flapper as the key female and fashion figure of the age is largely due to the fact that our conception of the Twenties has been heavily influenced and shaped by the moving image, by both the films made at the time and later cinematic interpretations.

In terms of film, the 1920s opened with Olive Thomas starring in 'The Flapper' as a naughty schoolgirl who falls from grace. The film cemented the link between the name, the look and the shocking identity of the flapper; a concept that was disseminated throughout the decade by amongst others Clara Bow in *The Plastic Age* and *It*; Louise Brooks in *Pandora's Box* and *Diary of a Lost Girl*; and Joan Crawford in *Our Dancing Daughters*. The flapper was young, boyish, had buckets of sex appeal, paraded around in shift dresses and fur coats, and wore cloche hats over her bobbed hair. It's that same flapper we're still having projected at us decades later in films such as *Thoroughly Modern Millie*, *Bugsy Malone*, and in endless television episodes of *Agatha Christie's Poirot*.

It is because she was so shocking and distinctive in comparison to her mother and grandmother, and because she represented the extremes of the new, more liberal post-World War I society, that she has become the predominant focus of so many studies of the 1920s. Too often any Twenties woman in a cloche hat, bobbed hair and make-up is labelled a flapper, and indeed many of the women in the photographs and drawings in this book have the look we associate with these temptress sirens – but one should not confuse a look with an attitude.

It's as much a cultural misunderstanding to think that all women in the 1920s dressed in close-fitting hats and bold, colourful beaded dresses, as it is to imagine that all women who did dress this way were flappers. For many, the wearing of these sack dresses and cloche hats and the adoption of a cropped hairstyle was simply and only an act of fashion.

It's important to acknowledge that what we see on the pages of this book are without exception the young dressed in the latest fashions. Just as today's fashion magazines do not represent accurately what the majority of the population looks like and how they dress, neither did magazines then. By definition fashion is only interested in the new, the luxurious and the beautiful. What we see on the pages of magazines then as now is an ideal. A mature woman in the 1920s was as unlikely to dress in a short beaded dress, as a mature woman now would indulge in the latest hot pants craze. Nevertheless, these images give us not only an idea of what the young were wearing, but they also provide an insight into the looks and beauty ideals women aspired to, and how these trickled down into mainstream fashions.

However, what is different about the Twenties is that it represents the first time in history when the printed press constitutes a more or less accurate representation and recording of what 'ordinary' young women wore – unlike in previous decades and centuries when representations were limited to the elite. High-end luxury fashion publications reserved for the wealthy were joined by hosts of cheaper women's magazines and fashion-oriented newspaper supplements aimed at lower income groups. Advances in printing techniques and a lowering of printing and publishing costs played an important part in this process.

12

Right
Green day dress, black dress with gauze
collar and chiffon dress with paisley
patterning – all by Berthe Hermance,
together with a pink dress with pleating
and a blue and white dress with
matching hat. *La Femme Chic*, 1923

More importantly, though, the 1920s saw the rise of what could be termed the 'democratisation' of fashion. For the first time in history, women who had been previously excluded from partaking in fashion for economic and practical reasons, were now allowed to indulge and incorporate fashionable dressing into their lives.

In terms of cause and effect, more women could afford fashion, so publications to 'aid' them in their purchasing choices appeared in droves. This desire for fashion at the lower levels of the market is also clearly noticeable in the much-expanded fashion sections of the 1920s mail-order catalogues of companies such as Sears, Roebuck & Co. and McCall's in the USA, and in the catalogues of the London-based department stores in the United Kingdom.

New Wardrobes for New Women

The main reason for this wider participation and interest in fashion can be attributed largely to the fact that the style of clothing women aspired to wear had simplified significantly from the elaborate pre-war haute couture gowns into fashions that were looser, more comfortable and, crucially, easier to make and copy. It would however be too restrictive to look at this democratisation only from a design point of view. The Great War, which ended only two years before the decade began, did precipitate changes and simplification in design due to material shortages; but all of these shifts were only really possible and acceptable because the idea of 'what a woman should be' was also shifting concurrently.

The war introduced many changes into the lives of women of all classes. Working-class women not only found themselves often solely in charge of the household, they were also catapulted from the kitchen sink to employment outside the home, and so were now often the principal breadwinners. Employment opportunities varied from posts in heavy industry, to driving ambulances or buses, to working in soup kitchens or taking on clerical roles. Of course, many women had worked prior to the war but their employment opportunities, such as domestic service, were very limited and, more often than not, gave them little responsibility or autonomy.

Many middle-class women experienced a similar change in experience and opportunity, and contrary to popular belief even upper-class women took on work – although this tended to be more genteel than the types of work their social inferiors were involved in. Not only did women perform vital tasks during the war, for the first time many experienced both social and financial freedom. Needless to say, in the post-war period women were not particularly inclined to meekly return to their previous domestic duties of baking and childrearing once their men came home.

This active employment of women also had wider social repercussions. Not only did they have more freedom in terms of finances and employment, social shifts were taking place both out of necessity and from changes in public attitude, which had a positive and liberating impact on women's lives.

By the 1920s, the city was no longer the exclusive domain of men, largely because the war had put an end to the chaperoning system. Previously, ladies of a certain class never did anything so disreputable as venture into a city alone; post-1918, etiquette and social mores had to be relaxed as women needed to be able to travel to work. The simple visibility of women in cities effected a change in attitude towards them from men – they were no longer the invisible domestic angels of earlier times, they were the women who had gone to work and kept the country going in times of crisis.

It also needs to be remembered that prior to the war, the suffragette movement had already gained momentum and that the end of the war saw women over the age of 30 granted the vote in Britain – with the USA following a year later. The 1920s would see a revival of women's demands for equal status culminating in the 'Flapper Vote' of 1928 that granted suffrage to all British women over the age of 21, giving them full equality with male voters. These changes were not only legislatively important, socially they granted women more recognition and gave them new freedoms. The press termed this newly liberated creature The New Woman.

This New Woman was heavily discussed in the contemporary press, indicating quite how much had changed. She was 'new' because she took on new roles and responsibilities, because she was no longer stuck at home, and because she was not simply going to shut up and return to her former life. This 'new' liberated woman needed and got a wardrobe to match – one of simpler, more comfortable elegance to correspond with her freer life.

The Fashionable Silhouette

By the start of the 1920s the fashionable female silhouette lacked structure, to the extent that dresses were often referred to as 'sacks', 'chemises', 'slips' or 'slip-overs', indicating the absence of a defined shape and the ease with which one put them on and took them off. This silhouette, which was radically different from the more traditional pre-war heavily-corseted Edwardian fashions, had developed out of the changes introduced by haute couturier, Paul Poiret. As early as 1907, he created a vogue for neo-classical empire line garments, which, instead of accentuating and enhancing curves, favoured a vertical silhouette. His designs abandoned the S-line corset; he himself hailed this as his triumph, however it needs to be noted that for the majority of women, save those with boyish narrow figures, this was simply replaced with straighter elasticated corsets that flattened curves and were not necessarily any more comfortable. By 1912 this straighter shape triumphed and could be seen in nearly all the Parisian couturiers' collections, and only the very old or old-fashioned had not adopted this modern, straighter look.

The change in garment length was also a process that started prior to the Twenties. Hemlines had crept up during the war in response to shortages and rationing; the straighter silhouette remained popular and developed into more architectural proportions for the same reason. By 1913 women were showing a little ankle; by 1918 fashionable dresses and coats had made their way up to calf length, which is where, with some minor variations, they would remain until around 1921 or 1922.

Whilst Poiret's pre-war creations introduced simplicity of silhouette, they were ultimately still very intricate, elaborate and extremely luxurious with regards to construction, materials and embellishment. Nevertheless his idea of simplifying female attire was taken up and taken to new levels by Gabrielle 'Coco' Chanel. She was a visionary designer in her own right but she also understood the new ideas and needs brought about by the war and translated these into dress.

Chanel grasped that the leisure classes who escaped to Biarritz and Deauville to sit out the war in style now had a greater need for comfortable yet elegant clothes as they discovered the joys of outdoor activities. For this reason, Chanel opened her first fashion boutique in Biarritz in 1915, presenting elegant leisurewear in jersey, a material formerly only used for workwear and undergarments. Chanel openly acknowledged her designs drew inspiration from servant girls, fishermen and ordinary workfolk. Her *pauvre chic* or 'poverty chic' fashions were a great success but one should not be fooled: her garments were anything but *pauvre*; they were exquisitely made and often lined in more luxurious material such as silk. Nevertheless, the changes she introduced to the silhouette were paramount to establishing the 1920s' fashionable shapes.

Another factor that contributed to the acceptance and popularity of more comfortable and simpler fashions was the fact women had to take on men's roles during the war: working in factories, driving buses and ambulances, and most importantly coming to the aid of the war industries. At work they were required to wear practical clothing that would not endanger them, so for many factory girls full knickers, a variation on bloomers, became their working uniform. These aptly named 'slack girls' would never have dreamt of wearing their work gear in public as it was purely utilitarian and, therefore, not only un-ladylike but also unfashionable. However the comfort introduced by these slacks was something that held great appeal, and something women were not about to abandon after the war.

Betty Solves
the
Housedress Problem
at Macy's

Left and right
Cover of Macy's mail order catalogue,
1923

A postcard of a young woman working
behind her Singer sewing machine, A
beaded dancing dress is displayed on
a dressmaker's dummy to her side.
c.1925.

What more and more of these young women were doing after work hours also had its impact on the need for comfort: dancing. The years just before, during and after World War I saw a growing interest and enthusiasm for dancing, but a far more energetic style of dancing than that of previous generations. Whilst traditional dances did not disappear, they were joined by new exotic styles such as the Tango, which had originated in Buenos Aires and required garments that allowed for higher and wider leg movements.

Another less credited yet no less important factor that influenced the development of freer styles was the growing impact and importance of avant-garde art movements. Artists frequently collaborated with fashion designers as fashion illustrators, textile designers and on actual fashion designs, but it was the ideas of these new and exciting art movements that really infused fashion with renewed dynamism and alternative approaches

and aesthetics; the Wiener Werkstätte, Russian Constructivism, Fauvism, Futurism, Cubism… in varying capacities all contributed to a rethinking of various aspects of fashion design including the simplified female silhouette. The Futurists, Constructivists and Cubists were the most influential in this context. Both the Russian and Italian avant-garde saw its involvement with fashion as an ideological engagement: fashion was part of a bigger social revolution and needed therefore to be rethought. Even though their ideology differed considerably in political terms, both Constructivist and Futurist artists conceptualised and designed garments for workers which were utilitarian yet original, and functional yet beautiful. The use of bold blocks of colour characterised designs of both movements and was derived from Cubist art; by using these blocks of contrasting colour, a need for a simpler cut was paramount as the body effectively became a canvas. Even though these utopian 'art' designs were rarely put into commercial production, they nevertheless functioned as a catalyst for debate about appropriate female attire. More importantly they also served as inspiration for designers who took on board the notion of 'the body as canvas', and went on to incorporate and popularise straighter female silhouettes into fashion.

So by the time we reach the Twenties, ideas of liberation, simplification and practicality were firmly established as the dominant fashion trend. Moreover, thanks to the popularisation of Chanel's leisurewear designs, comfort was no longer the antithesis of luxury, elegance and high fashion.

Vive Ste Anne

Lucia

Stylish Participation

This simplification of garment structure had two clear consequences, which directly impacted on the spread of fashionable clothing. Firstly, there was an exponential rise in home dressmaking, as women with little or even no experience could now tackle a dress project with relative ease and produce simple garments. Women's magazines aimed at the lower middle and upper working classes featured droves of adverts for dressmaking courses organised by a variety of private and public institutions. These adverts often featured illustrations of fashionable ladies carrying armfuls of garments accompanied with taglines such as, 'I made all these clothes myself quite easily and they cost me less than half the usual price'. The adverts not only played on women's desire to be part of fashion, but also the novelty of their ability to now be part of it. The use of slogans and articles explaining that home dressmaking was in fact a money-saving activity clearly shows that there was still anxiety and trepidation on the part of many women that fashion was frivolous and wasteful; something for the elite only and not for the likes of them. For that reason, the reassurance that being fashionable was morally acceptable had to be sold to women as a responsible domestic and economic act.

The second consequence of the silhouette simplification was the easier, high-volume production of ready-to-wear clothing. The war had greatly advanced production techniques as large volumes of quality uniforms had to be produced in small spaces of time. This knowledge and experience would be applied to the quickly growing ready-to-wear industry of the 1920s.

Sizing had also got somewhat better, although there was still no such thing as standard dress sizes and most manufacturers made up their own sizing system which was often based on little, inaccurate or no body data at all. However as fashions at the start of the Twenties were rather vertical and voluminous this was not an immediate problem – only later in the decade when dresses became more closely fitted to the torso did these inadequate sizing systems cause

problems and endless home alterations. Correct sizing and perfect tailoring remained the premise of haute couture, and whilst fashionable styles were now easier to copy, the perfect fit remained a marker of distinction.

Production & Consumption

The ready-to-wear industry flourished in the Twenties, especially in America through the development of national markets accessed through chain stores and mail order catalogues, and the impact of these cheaper, fashionable clothes was clearly felt.

In addition to these production developments the spread of new cheap, man-made fibres resembling satins and silks, allowed more women to consume the latest fashionable styles at a relatively low cost. In particular rayon, which had been developed and improved since the late 19th century and was known as art-silk (artificial silk) allowed the mimicking of a luxury fabric at low cost. This meant that both the handy housewife and ready-to-wear manufacturers could now copy silk garments previously reserved for the elite at a fraction of the cost.

Art-silk may not have felt like the real deal, but it looked sufficiently like silk to achieve a look of luxury and fashionability. Contemporary sources complained it was always a little too much on the wrong side of shiny, in particular when used for stockings, but the practical and fashionable young lady solved this problem by powdering her stockings with face or talcum powder. This not only shows ingenuity but also points to women's increasing engagement with, as well as knowledge and understanding of fashion.

Despite the huge growth in the ready-to-wear market, the 1920s did not see the disappearance of the middle-market's vogue for custom-made dresses. This section of the trade catered to ladies who wanted garments made to their size and specification, but who could not afford haute couture. Within the custom-made or couture business there were great differences in pricing bands. Those operating at the

Below left and right
A green silk evening dress with pointed
skirt panels. *How to Make Dresses
the Modern Singer Way*, The Singer
Company, c.1924

An orange and blue patterned tunic
dress, draped at the back and worn
over an orange wide-sleeved underslip.
Short Cuts to Home Sewing, The Singer
Sewing Company, c.1923

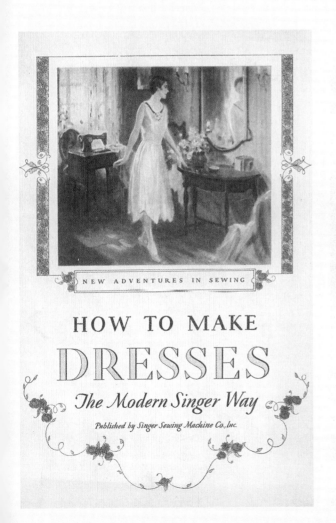

GRANDS MAGASINS DE LA SAMARITAINE

67 A 81, RUE DE RIVOLI, PONT-NEUF ET MONNAIE, PARIS

MANIÈRE DE PRENDRE LES MESURES

COSTUMES ET VÊTEMENTS POUR DAMES ET JEUNES FILLES

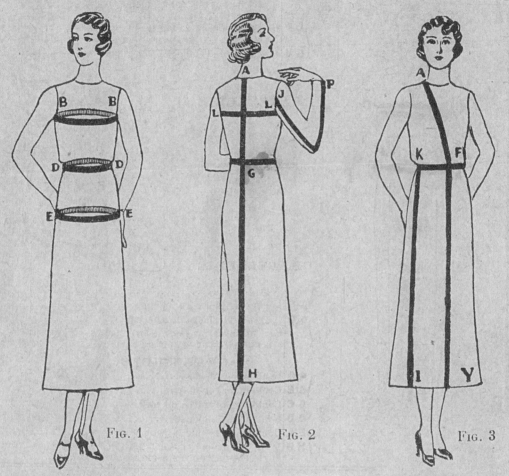

Fig. 1   Fig. 2   Fig. 3

Mesures de Madame ....

à ....   *département* ....

Fig.			M.	C.
1	**BB**	Contour entier du corps *sous les bras* à la partie la plus saillante de la poitrine		
1	**DD**	Tour de taille		
1	**EE**	Contour des hanches (0m15 au-dessous de la taille).		
2	**AG**	Longueur de taille derrière prise au bas du col.........		
2	**AGH** (1)	Longueur totale derrière, prise au bas du col. (*Indispensable pour les vêtements de fillettes*).		

Fig.			M.	C.
3	**AF**	Longueur de taille devant, prise à la couture de l'épaule.		
3	**FY**	Longueur de jupe, devant....		
2	**GH**	Longueur de jupe, derrière...		
3	**KI**	Longueur de jupe, sur le côté.		

CORSETS, GAINES, SOUTIEN-GORGE

Pour les mesures des Corsets, nous indiquer le tour de taille pris sur la chemise à la partie la plus mince.

Pour les Gaines, nous indiquer les mesures prises sur les hanches à l'endroit le plus fort.

Pour les Soutien-gorge, nous donner contour de

cheaper end of the scale mostly provided copies of Parisian models only, whilst at the top end of this market these copies were complemented with ranges of own in-house designs.

Only the elite could afford haute couture and, until the 1920s, even they mostly only relied on it for luscious evening wear; for everyday clothes such as street dresses, tea frocks and sportswear these women employed their local dressmaker. Postwar there was little demand for luxurious evening wear, so couturiers set out to supplant these seamstresses by designing entire wardrobes – from the overcoat down to the negligée. These wearable, everyday designs were less expensive than their previous offerings, and brought haute couture into the wealthy clientele's everyday dress. So even within the lofty world of haute couture, we see some sort of democratisation taking place.

However, the majority of women remained almost entirely reliant on home dressmaking – only buying new and ready-made items such as accessories, stockings and jewellery to finish off their outfits.

Paris – Capital of Fashion

Even though London and New York had a booming fashion industry fashions with a capital 'F' were set, if not dictated, by Paris. If a garment did not come from the French capital, it had to be inspired by a creation from the haute couture salons of Paris – otherwise, it simply wasn't fashion. The city was the epicentre of elegance and taste and had been the proprietor of all things luxurious and *de rigueur* since the court of King Louis XVI. This reputation was cemented in the 19th century by the establishment of haute couture as a creative industry by Charles Frederick Worth, who introduced seasonality and fashion collections, firmly linking art to commerce.

As true fashion could only originate in Paris, the elite travelled twice a year from all over the globe to purchase the latest fashions by their favoured haute couturiers. This fashionable set was joined by department store owners and ready-to-wear manufacturers, who also travelled far and wide to find out what their clients back home in Buenos

Aires, Havana or New York would be clambering for in the coming season. Copying had been a part of the haute couture industry from its beginnings, and fully aware that imitation would happen, Parisian maisons sold official models for duplication in an attempt to regulate and capitalise on this common practice. Bonded models were original couture garments, and were sold to manufacturers and retailers who used them as a source for line-for-line copies; toiles which were muslin models sold for similar purposes. The former were aimed at the upmarket department stores such as Harrods and Macy's, which advertised their lines as official Chanel, Patou and Lanvin models and copied the garment as closely as possible; the latter were aimed at the middle-market, ready-to-wear industry, which used them as inspiration for cheaper copies produced in high volume. The salons even offered paper patterns produced for the lower end of the same market, demonstrating that Parisian fashion was as much about artistry and design excellence as it was a well organised and profitable industry – an industry capitalising on its position and reputation.

The very word 'Parisian' was synonymous with all things luxurious, elegant and of good taste, and advertisers exploited this in every way possible. The emerging beauty and cosmetics industry relied heavily on its links – either real or imagined – with Paris, but equally products as banal as chocolate mints or diet pills could be turned into something exotic and special merely by adding the word Parisian into the advertising copy. In this way, through a simplification in silhouette, an organised ready-to-wear industry and new materials, Parisian couture, which had previously been exclusive to the upper classes and the elite, now trickled down to a far wider section of society.

Design & Decoration

If the change in silhouette was radical, the actual variety in designs – especially in decoration – was even more so. These new modes of dressing were not just looser, freer, more functional and thoroughly modern, but also revealed a range of influences and

Mlle PAULETTE DUVAL

Costume de Dœuillet

Left
The famous dancer and actress
Paulette Duval in a costume by
Doeuillet. Illustration by Vladimir
Barjansky. *Gazette du Bon Ton*, 1920

inspiration that drew on a wide variety of sources.

The opening decade of the 20th century saw the reintroduction of a vivid colour palette into fashion. Paul Poiret is credited as the first designer to embrace bright colours and present haute couture creations in jonquil yellows, electric blues, bright pinks and vivid greens. His inspiration for these brightly multicoloured creations came from the arts: the Fauvist painters had caused a stir at the 1905 Salon d'Automne with their non-naturalist colour palettes and quasi-expressionist style, and in 1909 the Ballets Russes had taken Paris by storm with their Oriental fantasies. Colour was in the arts and, as an avid art collector, Poiret wanted to elevate fashion to the same status by translating these contemporary artistic expressions into his creations. The resulting garments were bright, innovative and most of all luxurious.

The Ballets Russes' influence was not limited to colour but also crossed over into the stylistic development of fashion. Its style of Orientalism, best described as an imaginary mix of exotic influences from far-off times and places, could be clearly seen in Poiret's collections. The Orient, in this context, was not so much a geographical location as an imaginary idea. It encompassed areas of influence as diverse as South America, Africa and Asia, and did not limit itself to reality of time and place; rather it drew on ancient and often mythical histories and peoples to achieve its wide fantastical spectrum. The result of this Orientalist influence was that items such as harem trousers, kimono capes, turbans and tunics entered the fashionable Western wardrobe.

Whilst other couturiers quickly followed suit in abandoning the Edwardian pastel palette and outdated corseted styles in favour of these exotic, voluptuous and more fluid garments, Parisian haute couture initially continued to promote elitist and luxurious fashions. Consequently, this first shift had little impact on what the average woman wore. It was a reinterpretation of this Orientalism in the 1920s that trickled down to the woman in the street, and had a veritable and universal impact on women's style.

During the war, Poiret's fantastical 'One Thousand and One Nights' gowns went out of fashion, but the exotic element in these creations re-emerged in a more wearable and practical format: embellishment. So by the start of the 1920s, the exotic shapes explored by Poiret had shifted to the aforementioned altogether more flat, square and straight dresses, but with an abundance of Oriental detailing ranging from Chinese and Russian folk embroideries, African- and South American-inspired motifs, kimono-style sleeves and coats, opulent beading and tassels of imagined slave dresses, Oriental-inspired jewelled turbans and headbands, marabou feather fans and capes, compacts and cigarette holders in bold colours and motifs…

Africa, or at least an imagined Eurocentric version of it, provided a rich source of inspiration in the form of tribal prints, arm cuffs and chunky costume jewellery. A driving force behind contemporary art movements, the continent also made its appearance in fashion. Paris was entranced by Josephine Baker's banana skirt, while Chez Bricktop, a nightclub owned by African American vaudevillian star, Ada 'Bricktop' Smith, was the hottest ticket in town. Jazz and dances born in the African American community, such as the Lindy Hop and Charleston, were considered the height of modernity. Paris was under the spell of these creations, and naturally fashion followed suit.

Another African source of inspiration came from Ancient Egypt. It had been a source of inspiration prior to the Twenties, but after Howard Carter's 1922 discovery of Tutankhamun's tomb the world was caught up in Egyptomania. Cinemas built to resemble Ancient Pharaonic temples, Singer sewing machines decorated with lotus and sphinx motifs, fashions with hieroglyphic patterns, over-the-top costume jewellery 'resembling' the spoils discovered in the death chamber, lotus flower embroideries, bicorne and tricorne Egyptian hats with an albeit vague resemblance to Pharaonic headdress. The Egyptian obsession can also be seen in a stylistic shift in fashion illustration, as several high-end publications temporarily adopted an Egyptian perspective by depicting models in profile against a flat background.

Right
Advertisement for Madeleine Vionnet.
L'Illustration des Modes, 1920

madeleine vionnet

ROBES MANTEAUX FOURRURES

222, RUE DE RIVOLI, PARIS (FACE AUX TUILERIES) TÉLÉPHONE CENTRAL 24·04

Thayaht.19

Madeleine VIONNET montre sa nouvelle collection de Robes, Manteaux, Fourrures depuis le 1er Octobre.

Right
A postcard of the Hollywood actress
Pola Negri wearing a fur-trimmed
Russian-inspired coat with peasant-style
embroidery, c.1921

The vogue for Russian embroideries was also rooted in a cultural development. The result of the 1917 Russian Revolution was the arrival of over 150,000 Russian émigrés in Paris, many of whom would end up either setting up their own couture houses or working for established Parisian houses. Many of the women had learnt embroidery in their childhood, and soon a fashion for these vivid embellishments was established – not least as they offered a substitute for luxurious fabrics in the immediate post-war years. But the Russian influence could be seen in other developments too. Taking their cue from the *kosovorotka*, a traditional embroidered men's tunic, the Russian houses such as Kitmir, Irfe and Yteb created a distinctive garment for women that became extremely sought after. The Russians also introduced Paris to their traditional fur and fabric combinations that would become a classic on blouses, dresses and coats in the Twenties Their most lasting impact, however, would be on headgear through the *kokoshnik*, a traditional Russian headdress, which together with the cloche hat would come to epitomise Twenties fashions.

Historic styles continued to inspire designers too, though our view of the decade has been shaped by the modernity and innovation of the racier creations. The most important and popular example is the 'picture dress', a long dress with a wide, hooped infanta skirt, attached to a fitted bodice. The dress first made its appearance in the previous decade but remained a favourite of older women, and was seen as a more feminine alternative to the younger, straighter styles.

In terms of the colours used by designers, it is nearly impossible to speak of a single colour that defines the decade. A clear distinction between day and evening wear is possible; the latter saw a wide variety from the brightest pinks, yellows, greens and blues, whilst the former favoured more conservative colours such as dark browns, greys, blues and black. That said, bright red, green and orange daywear also existed. A class distinction can also be observed: a working woman's wardrobe, whilst featuring fashionable styles, came in safer neutral and darker colours as her clothes had to last longer and could

not fall victim to the whims of fashion. Brighter colours were nevertheless introduced in the form of accessories such as hats, gloves, bags and scarves, items that could be updated to fall in line with the fashions of the day at a relatively low cost. There was, of course, also a seasonal divide with summer clothes being lighter in colours and materials.

A Twenties fashion colour that deserves closer attention is black. Whilst often the popularity for black is attributed to Chanel's little black dress of 1926, the picture is somewhat more complex. American *Vogue* in 1926 described her LBD as the Chanel Model T, predicting it would become a universal uniform for women. However, black was fashionable before the 1920s – especially for daywear. It was still the mourning colour but not exclusively. And as the images in this book demonstrate, the widespread enthusiasm for simple black dresses in both upper- and middle-market publications dispels the myth that only after Chanel launched her LBD was it possible for women of all classes to copy it and turn it into a universal uniform. In fact, evidence hints very clearly that black was more than likely a staple of working and lower middle class wardrobes, both as work and fashionable wear before the elite adopted it. As *The New Republic: A Journal of Opinion* observed as early as July 1921, 'So for street wear especially, we have throngs of females black from head to foot.'

Favoured fabrics still included rich silks, velvets, embroidered nets, and woven gold and silver lamé at the top end of the market; these were mostly reserved for eveningwear. This list was however joined by other more comfortable and practical fabrics such as jersey, mohair, gabardine, crêpe, kasha and rayon, which directly reflects the freer urban lifestyle enjoyed by women.

Sportswear

Women also saw the introduction of various 'new' garments, best described as sportswear, into their wardrobes. Initially only for members of the elite, the influence of these types of clothes nevertheless trickled down to less well-off consumers.

POLA NEGRI

LA MODE·SPORT

Printemps-Eté 1929

Sportswear is by far the most important type of attire to impact on women's lives in the Twenties. This is true in two distinct yet related ways. As already stated, the privileged echelons of society had discovered the joys of outdoor pursuits during the war, and new garments had been developed to cater to these new hobbies. This was particularly true for women; their new and more liberated social status allowed their increased engagement in athletic pursuits. Prior to this, sports such as golfing, skating, hunting, skiing and riding had not excluded female participation, but women had always undertaken these activities in clothes that were in keeping with the feminine ideal of the time. Not only did this mean they had to wear uncomfortable and restrictive gowns, they actually wore corsets underneath these 'sports' ensembles.

The late 1910s and the 1920s saw a host of new, more comfortable interpretations of female sportswear. Indebted to Chanel's introduction of jersey and her use of male tailoring, and to the social shifts which had 'freed' women from some of the more restrictive regulations of pre-war times, these changes were now clearly reflected in the new style and comfort of women's general attire – but most particularly in their sports wardrobes.

The modern sportswear wardrobe saw the introduction of altogether new garments such as motoring and even flying fashions, as the modernity of cars and airplanes was reflected in emerging styles. High-end fashion publications featured women descending from cars in long woollen and leather coats, accessorized with the latest in glove and headgear design. Indeed the motor industry particularly targeted the modern women and there appeared endless adverts of women driving cars, at once affirming their 'new' status and propagating the modernity of the female body.

These sports fashions, whilst often being just fashions, nevertheless reveal that the post-war years saw an increasing interest in matters of health for both men and women. Physical education in schools was becoming a more important part of the curriculum, while local and national sports clubs grew in membership. Even though there was still

Left
Four golfing outfits, France. *La Mode-Sport*, c.1928 – a two-piece jersey ensemble with appliqué initials, a beige Kasha dress, a dress of dark blue crêpe with a printed scarf, and a black skirt worn with a yellow jersey jumper.

Right
Jantzen swimwear advertisement – the
suit that changed bathing to swimming.
Liberty magazine, 1929

a clear gender difference in terms of which sports were taught and marketed to men and women, the overriding health discourse meant women were actively encouraged to partake in a much wider variety of physical activities than in previous decades.

Health had been pushed onto the agenda by medical advances but the shocking figures that in 1917 only 36% of the men examined were suitable for full military duties and that 40% were entirely unfit or classified as unable to undergo physical exertion, probably had a much greater impact on this drive for health. A need for a healthy nation was paramount especially as the 1920s wore on, and the early signs that World War I may not have been 'the war to end all wars' were starting to appear. Indeed this renewed cult of the body beautiful would take on extremely sinister connotations in Germany in the following decade. It would appear that the interest in sports and its accompanying new fashions has to been seen in a much wider social and political context to grasp its full importance.

Another sport that became incredibly popular, particularly with women, was swimming. Women had been allowed to swim in the Olympic Games of 1912, and from there on the sport grew in popularity – especially during the second half of the 1920s after Miss Gertrude Ederle's 1926 swim across the English Channel beat the record by two hours. Even more impressive, when you consider that at the time, the record was held by a man.

This official Olympic seal of approval for swimming as a female-friendly sport was a catalyst for the development of a more modern and practical women's swimming costume. The Edwardian culottes and skirt combination was replaced in the 1920s with woollen jersey sleeveless tank suits, reminiscent of earlier male swimming costumes. These semi-elasticated garments came in a wide variety of colours and patterns, and were infinitely more suited to water pursuits than their historic counterparts. As the swimwear company Jantzen declared in its advertising slogan of 1929, this was 'the suit that changed bathing into swimming'.

This dramatic redesign of women's swimwear was only possible because ideas about women and

modesty had shifted considerably in line with the other cultural developments previously highlighted. This more liberal attitude by society to women and their bodies was also reflected in a related cultural phenomenon – the exponential rise in the number of outdoor public swimming pools in the inter-war years.

Public pools had become features of most larger cities in the 19th century due to increasing health and hygiene concerns. Initially these were reserved for men only, and even when they opened their doors to women, pools for both sexes were segregated to the extent that each even had a separate entrance to the pool buildings. Mixed bathing was introduced in several locations as early as 1901, but did not become acceptable practice until much later – indeed, certain ponds and pools did not allow it until the 1930s. It was the lidos that proliferated in the 1920s that both propagated and affirmed the positive shifts in gender division, as the majority allowed mixed bathing and were marketed as family spaces. The modern woman in her modern swimming costume became an icon of the era. The Bathing Belle, who could be found anywhere from travel posters advertising seaside resorts to Hollywood films, was hailed as an aspirational figure and the popularity of her look increased that of swimming.

Beauty Ideals

Another factor that contributed to the fashion for outdoor bathing locales and the need for less restrictive and modest swimming costumes was the vogue for sunbathing. Whilst for centuries tanned skin had been shunned by the elite as a sign of poverty and low status, the new interest in outdoor pursuits saw a major shift in this, and suntans came to be considered not only a sign of good health, but also a fashionable look. The mode for tans can also be linked to the appearance of dresses with plunging backs, sleeveless gowns and the rising of hemlines. The more the body was on display, the more it had to be groomed and disciplined.

Another body discipline that is linked to the vogue for athletic participation and health awareness was the rise of dieting. Whilst as late as 1917 adverts for

Blonde, brunette or titian . . . there are certain Jantzen colors best suited to your type. Once you've chosen yours, 'tis a simple matter to complete your ensemble . . . robe, cap, belt, shoes . . . for beach parade.

Then, when cool waters beckon, cast aside your robe and enjoy the full pleasure of swimming in a Jantzen. Tightly knitted from the strongest, long-fibred wool, a Jantzen fits you perfectly, permits such freedom for swimming that you scarcely know its on you! Smart, too, in appearance, with its trim, youthful lines.

See the new models at your favorite store . . . the *Twosome, Sun-suit, Speed-suit.* Many are conveniently buttonless in all *sizes*—others without buttons up to 42. Specially packed in «color harmony sets» for each type. Gay hues, pastel shades, or stripes. Color-fast. Your weight is your size. Jantzen Knitting Mills, Portland, Oregon; Vancouver, Canada; Sydney, Australia.

Jantzen

The suit that changed
bathing to swimming

COPYRIGHT BY
KODAK LTD BY E

'stoutening' pills and creams can be found in ladies magazines, the '20s silhouette was slender and virtually curve-less. Some younger women naturally possessed this boyish shape, but for the majority elasticated de-emphasising corsets and dieting had to lend a helping hand. Fashion is never just about clothes; they need a body to animate them. In this way, to explore fashion is to explore the intimate relationship between body and fabric. By examining the design and style of clothes we can read the beauty ideals of any given time, as clothing is always designed with the ideal body in mind. In the 1920s, it's apparent only a slender frame would do: the lack of tailoring around the waist, later the dropped waist, the flat dresses that hid the breasts... the ideal body of the period was definitely slender and boyish.

This boyish frame was set off with the boyish haircut that has come to symbolise the era – the cropped bob. Women had cut their hair short at various points in history but these had always been short-lived trends rather than prolonged general fashions. Long hair is seen as a marker of femininity; its cutting off therefore is often interpreted as political. It is not clear who started the fashion, but what is certain is that it was not an overnight change, but a slower process. It started with a softer waved cut in the opening decade of the century and transmuted into, at its most extreme, an angular short bob closely cut to the skull in the mid 1920s. Furthermore, there was no single defining 'bobbed' haircut – many women cut their hair short, but the variety of bobs was wide. Initially men and older generations were horrified by this trend, but very quickly it became the accepted beauty ideal featured in both upmarket and cheap fashion publications – although it is worth noting that the images produced for the lower end of the market mostly featured the softer, less shocking variety of the haircut.

Both at the time and in retrospective histories, this fashion is seen as women adopting male traits. In the contemporary press the issue was heavily discussed and was seen as a quasi-assault on masculinity and a loss of femininity. More conservative papers saw this as such a threat and a symbol of doom that they proclaimed this would be the end of women cooking and looking after their men. For some this may have been a political statement; for others it was a haircut that suited their new freer lifestyles. For most it was just fashion.

The bob was the perfect cut for the cloche, or indeed the cloche was the perfect hat for the bob. The cloche, with its deep crown and small brim, was worn pulled down very low over the eyes and has become, like the bob, a defining characteristic of the era. Contrary to popular belief, though, it was not a Twenties 'invention' but had been worn since the mid-teens. Equally it was far from the only 'type' of headgear donned by fashionable woman. In fact, the opening years of the decade saw a plethora of different styles including bicorne and tricorne hats, turbans, Chinese toques, the Russian *kokoshnik* and a whole host of fantastical Oriental creations often combining two different types of headgear into one – such as turbans embroidered with *kokoshnik*s, or cloches with bicornes. The only linking feature was that most were, like the cloche, worn very low over the head. Throughout the decade hats took on semi-sculptural proportions, and the existing variety was joined by new creations. These include the tightly fitted casque, which was derived from racing helmets, and the beret. Previously reserved for children and the working classes, the beret saw itself transformed into a fashion item – often accessorized with a flechette brooch.

Bobs and deep hats framed the face and turned it into a canvas. To accentuate and indeed complete the modern look, another new trend needs to be considered: visible make-up. Whilst previous generations had experimented with make-up, they had used it to bring out their natural beauty – that is to say to hide flaws – chic make-up was soft, pale and natural. The fashionable Twenties girl however wore a rather different face. Lips were coated in brightly coloured lipstick; eyes made up with dark eyeshadows and cheeks powdered with rouge. Prior to this, visible make-up had been the province of chorus girls and prostitutes; it was considered vulgar and its wearer of low status.

This changed dramatically with the growing popularity of Hollywood films. Early lighting was so bright that stars had to wear make up to accentuate their features so their faces could be clearly seen on screen. This was exceptionally important before the arrival of the talkies in the late 1920s as facial expressions had to convey emotion and narrative in lieu of dialogue. As film developed from short stories to full-blown features with more complex storylines, the stars of the silver screen became aspirational icons whose looks were copied worldwide. Max Factor, a Polish cosmetician, chemist and wigmaker soon developed a business empire, which not only provided the film industry but women worldwide with his cosmetics. Fancy powder compacts and lipstick holders in abstract art deco designs appeared on the market and were a must-have in the fashionable woman's purse.

Other accessories that could be procured quite cheaply included bracelets, clips, necklaces and earrings in coloured Bakelite or paste and diamanté. These cheap accessories were the perfect way of adding a touch of glamour to a home-made dress. Shoes also came in a wide and exciting variety of colour, cut and embellishment. Rising hemlines meant legs and feet were now on display and so shoes became a focal point. The majority of shoes were high heeled and styles included T-bars and crossover straps. Leather, brocades, silks, gold and silver kid and a host of embellishments including embroideries in silks, beading, painted designs and diamanté clips and straps turned footwear into 'foot jewellery'. Like hats and other accessories, a pair of fashionable shoes was the perfect way to update an outfit. So from head to toe women could incorporate new and exciting shapes, colours, patterns and designs into what they were wearing.

Whilst often highly mythologised and at times misinterpreted, 1920s fashions have earned their right to be remembered and celebrated, not least because of their spectacular nature, beauty, variety and novelty. They are the sartorial embodiment of a society in change; a change that greatly benefitted women and saw significant steps in their social, economic and political liberation. This New Woman deserved nothing less than a 'new' wardrobe to accompany and represent her 'new' life. The different motifs of the new-found freedoms are all contained within the pages of this stylish book, which presents a record of the plethora of choices on offer to her in arguably the most iconic decade of the 20th century. The Twenties were about so, so much more than flappers and cloche hats.

Right and next page
Four hat designs by Parisian milliner
Jeanne Vivet. *Trés Parisien*, 1926

Drawing of various ensembles by Jean
Patou. *L'Illustration des Modes*, 1922

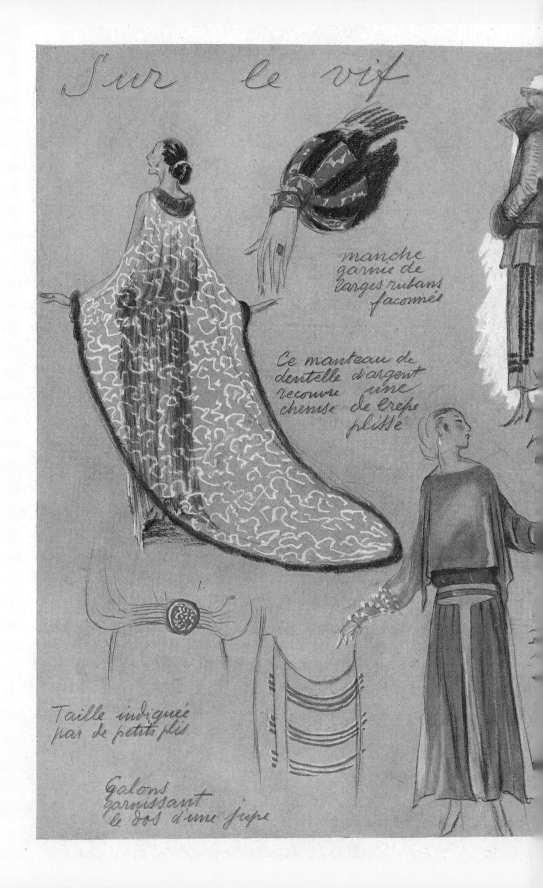

Sur le vif

manche
garnie de
larges rubans
façonnés

Ce manteau de
dentelle d'argent
recouvre une
chemise de crêpe
plissé

Taille indiquée
par de petits plis

Galons
garnissant
le dos d'une jupe

chez Jean Patou

décolleté en
crêpe froncé
et uni —

Pour l'auto:
manteau
de peau de
daim marron

Robe de crêpe
Georgette blanc
brodée   de
perles - Ruban
à la Taille

leur de
nègre et
T. de
—

ettes de
garnissent
n de cette
rêpe
t 2 tons

Grande robe du
soir en satin noir
et broché d'argent

Un
amusant
bas de
manche

Pinces liserées
d'agneau
assortie au col

1920s Daywear

Above
Woman in a green housecoat with
a draped hood, and rope and tassel
detail. *La Mode*, 1920

Above
Woman in a green day dress.
La Mode, 1920

Above and right
Woman in a black coat with a high-
buttoned collar. *La Mode*, 1920

A woman in a green dress with
short bell sleeves and a fur collar.
La Mode, 1920

Daywear

Le N° : 50 Cent.   24ᵉ Année. -- N° 47 -- 14 Novembre 1920   ★ ★ ★ -- 24 pages

Rédactrice en chef :
COUSINE JEANNE

**ON S'ABONNE SANS FRAIS
DANS TOUS LES BUREAUX DE POSTE**
Prix des abonnements

Hôtel du PETIT JOURNAL
61, rue Lafayette
PARIS

FRANCE ET COLONIES		UNION POSTALE	
7 francs	3 mois	8 francs	
13 francs	6 mois	14 francs	
25 francs	Un an	27 francs	

Below
'Jouerai-je?' (Should I play?), dress for
the races by Beer. Illustration by Pierre
Brissaud. *Gazette du Bon Ton*, 1920

Right
'Un Peu Beaucoup' (A little, a lot), two
day dresses. Illustration by Fernand
Simeon. *Gazette du Bon Ton*, 1920

UN PEU

BEAUCOUP

Right
'La belle Journée' (The glorious day),
summer dress by Paul Poiret. Illustration
By George Lepape. *Gazette du Bon
Ton*, 1920

LA BELLE JOURNÉE

Robe d'été, de Paul Poiret

Les jolis modèles en soie.

Paris-Blouses

Reproduction interdite

HIVER 1920-1921

Supplément au N° 11

Gaston DROUET, Éditeur.

6, Rue Ventadour, PARIS (1er arrᵗ)

Above and right
Selection of belted silk blouses.
Paris Blouses, 1920

Four 'practical housecoats'.
Paris Blouses, 1920

Daywear

3205   3206

3207

3208

PL. 10

Quelques Peignoirs Pratiques.

ÉTÉ 1920

Gaston DROUET, Editeur

Paris - Blouses.

Supplément au N°10

6, Rue Ventadour, PARIS (1ᵉʳ arrᵗ)

Reproduction interdite.

Above
The actress Norma Shearer wearing a
three-piece spring suit made of 'Spiral
Spun' and 'Moon-Glo' crêpe, c.1920

Right
Five casaque designs.
Paris Élégant, 1920

9782

9785

9784

9783

9786

PL.1098

GASTON DROUET, Editeur

6, Rue Ventadour, PARIS

Robe et blouses légères pour l'Été.

Paris Elégant

Reproduction interdite

Supplément au N°130-1920

Right
Selection of belted silk blouses.
Paris Blouses, 1920

3494

3495

3496

3497

3498

Les jolis effets de broderie.

Paris-Blouses.

Reproduction interdite.

HIVER 1920 1921   PL 3

Supplément au N° 11

Gaston DROUET, Éditeur.

6, Rue Ventadour, PARIS (1er arrt)

Above and right
Five casaque designs.
Paris Élégant, 1920

'Voici L'orage' (Here comes the storm),
afternoon dress by Paul Poiret. Illustration
by George Lepape. *Gazette du Bon Ton*,
1920

Daywear

Right
'Les Voila!' (There they are!),
two summer dresses by Doeuillet.
Gazette du Bon Ton, 1920

LES VOILA !

Robes d'Été, de Dœuillet

Above and right
A woman in a black skirt and a red
Russian blouse with a high neck and
ornamental buttons. *La Mode*, 1920

Embroidered taffeta dress with
red bow by Jeanne Lanvin.
L'Illustration des Modes, 1920

Daywear

MONNAIE
DU
PAPE
une
robe
de
Jeanne
LANVIN

Robe de taffetas noir brodée de soie blanche   ruban de taffetas qui garnit le côté est repris
et de paillettes de nacre. Le grand nœud de   sous la jupe beaucoup plus longue derrière (59).

Right
A cream tunic dress with black
embroidery worn over a green
underdress with wide embellished
sleeves. *Les Modèles Chics*, c.1920

Right
Grey crêpe de Chine dress by Chéruit,
navy blue and black dress by Jeanne
Lanvin, and orange and white dress by
Worth. Illustration by Pierre Brissaud,
L'Illustration des Modes, 1920

Below and right
A young woman in a summer ensemble of a pink pleated skirt and a red belted blouse. *La Mode*, 1921

Four designs for blouses by the Princesse Baratoff. *La Femme Chic*, 1921

La Mode

Rédactrice en Chef   COUSINE JEANNE

N° 29. — 17 Juillet 1921. 24 Pages -- 50 Centimes.

Découper dans ce Numéro le Bulletin de Vote pour le Concours des Préférences.

Previous page
Five afternoon dresses by Drecoll,
Elise Poret and Martial et Armand,
La Femme Chic, c.1921

Right
Day dress with wide black silk
sleeves worn with wide-brimmed
hat and buckled shoes. *Journal
des Demoiselles*, 1921

Daywear

A. Thiéry, Directeur

79, Boulev. Saint-Germain, PARIS

Le Gérant : Baeurlé

Above and right
A woman wearing a red patterned
dress with bell sleeves and a twisted
belt. *La Mode*, 1922

Designs for day dresses.
The Delineator, 1922

Daywear

Dress 3635

Dress 3633

Dress 3620
Embroidery design 10957

*Other views of these garments
are shown on page 105*

Dress 3639

Dress 3604

Previous page
Five silhouettes for a 'reception at the villa'. Dresses and coats are calf length and long handkerchief sleeves are favoured although, as the Soeurs Boue model reveals, shorter lace sleeves were also fashionable. The black coat and dress dispel the myth that black at this stage was still only worn whilst in mourning, and instead show that black was a fashion colour well before Coco Chanel introduced her 'Little Black Dress' in 1926. *La Femme Chic*, c.1922

Below
Designs for summer dresses.
The Delineator, 1922

Dress 3850

Blouse 3837
Skirt 2989
Embroidery
design 10972

Blouse 3632
Dress 3822

Dress 3844

Below
Designs for summer dresses.
The Delineator, 1922

*Other views and descriptions
are on page 89*

Dress 3861

Dress 3881

Dress 3864

Dress
3877

76

Below and right
Two women in winter dresses.
Le Petit Echo de La Mode, 1922

Matching blouse and skirt
ensemble by Pierce Tex. Underwood
and Underwood, c.1922

Notre Calendrier

Lundi .... 30 Janvier Sᵗᵉ Bathilde.
Mardi .. .. 31 — Sᵗᵉ Marcelle.
Mercredi.. .. 1ᵉʳ Février Sᵗ Ignace.
Jeudi .. .. 2 — Purification.
Vendredi.. .. 3 — Sᵗ Blaise.
Samedi.. .. 4 — Sᵗ Gilbert.
Dimanche .. 5 — Sᵗᵉ Agathe.

CHEZ SOI

ROBE en velours, garnie d'astrakan. Corsage kimono, à taille longue drapée sur une jupe froncée bordée d'astrakan. Corsage 13095, métrage : 2 m. 25 en 110. Jupe 13096, métrage : 2 m. 60 en 110.
ROBE en serge unie et serge écossaise. Fond de robe en serge écossaise avec tablier et panneau derrière en serge unie. Manches pagode à revers de serge unie. Corsage 13097, métrage : 1 m. 20 en 120 ; écossais, 1 m. 20 en 120. Jupe 13098, métrage : 1 m. 60 en 120 ; écossais, 2 m. 60 en 120.

Blouse Style "N"—Skirt Style "S"

Underwood & Underwood

CHARTREU
(ROBE DE MAISO

Left
Chartreux (Carthusian) 'House' day dress. The name of the dress refers to the similarities with the white hooded habit worn by monks of the Carthusian order. Illustration by David. *Gazette du Bon Ton*, 1922

Below
Dress Immaculée Conception (Immaculate Conception). The model is wearing a Russian-inspired headdress and the blue flowers sash refers to the colour of the Virgin Mary. *Gazette du Bon Ton*, 1922

N° 10 de La Gazette
Année 1922. — Croquis N° III

IMMACULÉE · CONCEPTION
(XVIIIe SIÈCLE)

Below and right
Day dress with matching hat
by Germaine. *L'Illustration des
Modes*, 1922

Abbé (Abbot) walking dress.
Illustration by David. *Gazette
du Bon Ton*, 1922

LE PIGEONNIER VERT
Robe de plein air de GERMAINE

David

Below

Blouses by Ruffie. The Venetian
backdrop of the top images lends
an air of luxury and travel to the
fashions. The top right blouse is adorned
with traditional inspired 'Russian'
embroideries whilst the top left model
takes its inspiration from ancient South
American motifs. All examples have
kimono-like sleeves. *La Femme Chic*,
c.1922

Above
Four blouses by Liberty.
La Femme Chic, c.1923

Dress 3647
Hat 3665
Embroidery design 10787

Dress 3651
Hat 3665

Dress 3610

Dress 3653
Embroidery design 10895

Dress 3625
Embroidery design 10918

Dress 3569

Cape 3602
Dress 3657
Hat 3325

Dress 3616
Embroidery design 10916

Other views and descriptions of these garments are shown on page 104

Left and above
Designs for summer dresses.
The Delineator, 1922

White and black satin frock worn
by Hollywood actress Eleanor
Boardman, c.1922

Daywear

Below
Selection of casaquins and blouses.
Le Petit Echo de la Mode, 1922

CASAQUE en voile imprimé, ornée de rubans de satin au col et en bordure des manches. Casaque 14233, métrage : 1 m. 50 en 100. — CASAQUE en crêpe de coton, garnie de ruban ciré passé en troutrou. Casaque 14234, métrage : 1 m. 60 en 100. — PALETOT en molleton, orné de galon et de broderies. Jupe droite.

Paletot 14235, métrage : 2 mètres en 120. Jupe 14236, métrage : 2 m. 50 en 120. — CASAQUE en crêpe marocain, garnie d'un col et d'un biais en taffetas. Casaque 14237, métrage : 2 mètres en 100. — CASAQUE en jersey de soie uni et rayé. Casaque 14238, métrage : 1 m. 20 en 110 ; tissu rayé, 0 m. 50 en 120.

Les meilleurs romans pour la famille et les jeunes filles sont édités dans la Collection "STELLA". Il paraît deux volumes par mois.

Below
Ensemble for the countryside by
Margaine Lacroix consisting of a sailor's
collar blouse and a pleated skirt. *La
Femme Chic*, c.1923

Below
Ensemble for the countryside by
Margaine Lacroix consisting of a sailor's
collar blouse and a pleated skirt. *La
Femme Chic*, c.1923

Left
Left
A model in a bengaline creation – a
woven ribbed man-made fibre ensemble,
heavily embroidered with peasant
inspired motifs and trimmed with fine
lace around the collar and cuffs, c.1923

Above
Black satin day dress embroidered in
yellow on the pockets and around the
hem, while the shoes are of black kid
and the hat is a black wide-brimmed
cloche. USA, c.1923

Daywear

Photograph of a model wearing a
Parisian floral crêpe de Chine gown.
Berlin, c.1923

White skirt and blouse ensemble.
The blouse has lace inserts and is
decorated with a diamante clip, while
the calf length skirt is finely pleated.
The model wears a slave bracelet on her
upper arm. USA, c.1923

92

Van Ultra

Dress Style 30-A

Underwood & Underwood

Left and Below
Rayon jersey sportswear ensemble
by Van Ultra. Underwood and
Underwood Photography, c.1923

Rayon jersey dress with sailor
collar by Van Ultra. Underwood and
Underwood Photography, c.1923

Dress Style 29 B

Van Ultra

Underwood & Underwood

94

Below
Four blouse designs with embroidered
detailing by Maison Caro. *La Femme
Chic*, c.1923

Right
A taffeta dress with pleated side panel
and extensive satin and lace trimmings.
Shown at the Auteuil races, 1923

Above
Four blouses by André Schwab, all
with extensive embroidered detailing.
La Femme Chic, c.1923

E 119205. ROBE en crêpe marocain ou en serge, ornée de
soutaches formant plastron sous un col Claudine fermé par un ruba
Corsage à taille longue et jupe froncée sous la ceinture. *Métrage :*
en 100. Cette robe se coupe sur notre patron-modèle 119205, av
figurine et explications ; taille 44. (Franco, 1 fr. 50 ; étranger, 1 fr
    E 119206. ROBE en gabardine, ornée de tresses piquées. Form
longue. Manches collantes, à poignets, en entonnoir. Petit col r
brodé ou de soie blanche. *Métrage : 3 m. 25 en 120.* Cette robe se
sur notre patron-modèle 119206, avec plan, figurine et explication:
44. (Franco, 1 fr. 50 ; étranger, 1 fr. 75.)
    E 119207. ROBE en crêpe de Chine ou maroklaine. Forme
avec ornements de ganses au plastron, à la ceinture et aux h
Métrage : 3 m. 35 en 110. Cette robe se coupe sur notre patron-
119207, avec plan, figurine et explications ; taille 44. (Franco, 1
étranger, 1 fr. 75.)
    E 119208. MANTEAU en velours de laine, garni de fourrure
toque russe en velours et fourrure assortie. *Métrage : 3 m. 60 e*
Ce manteau se coupe sur notre patron-modèle 119208, avec plan,

Above
Three women in long day dresses.
Le Petit Echo de la Mode, 1924

Daywear

Above and right
Tan silk afternoon dress with
a gathered lapel detail at the
waist, c.1924

Selection of summer dresses, Printemps
catalogue, 1924

Next page
Selection of summer dresses, Printemps
catalogue, 1924

Daywear

Robes

ÉTÉ 1921

66944.
ROBE
en marocain
de coton, cerise
mauve, saumon, citron,
brodée blanc et en
blanc, brodée noir
69 fr.
En jersey laine, grise,
castor, marine et noire,
brodée noir. .... 89 fr.
En jersev laine. gris. castor. marine.

66941. ROBE en crépon
coton, fond nattier, bois,
amande, et noir, impression
blanche.
La robe ...... 59 fr.

En tissu éponge, uni, mauve
nattier, citron, cerise, gris,
abricot et blanc... 45 fr.
En jersey laine uni, coloris
garnie ton opposé. 89 fr.
En damier pure laine, noir
et blanc, garnie galon et

66943. ROBE en tissu
éponge, garnie blanc, manches courtes, coloris 55 fr.
du 66941. *La robe.*
En serge, marine ou noire;
garnie de couleur 69 fr.
En jersey laine, uni, garniture couleur, coloris 95 fr.
du 66941. *La robe.*
En jersey laine jaspé, fond
marine, noir, canard, nègre
et bois. *La robe*.......... 135 fr.

66942. ROBE en voile de coton, fileté
quadrillé, mauve, cerise, citron, 45 fr.
nattier. *La robe* non doublée.
La robe doublée............ 59 fr.
En voile de coton fantaisie, fond marine,
nattier, mauve, cerise et noir impression
blanche. Non doublée....... 59 fr.
Doublée................. 75 fr.
En voile uni, mauve, corail, citron;
nattier. amande et blanc, 49 fr.
La robe non doublée ......
Doublée................. 63 fr.
En crêpe de Chine, marine, écaille, gris,

12

Robes

Au Printemps
paris

66945. **ROBE** en crépon fin, fond blanc brodé mauve, cerise, citron, nattier, noir, ou tout blanc, garniture couleur. *La robe* **69** fr.
En voile de coton fond écru, cerise, gris, impression couleur ou blanc, impression noire.
La robe, **69** f.
non doublée
La robe doublée .... **85** fr.
En foulard marine ou noir, dessins blancs. **110** fr.
En jersey soie fond beige, blanc, crème imprimé noir, ou marine imprimé gris. **135** fr.
La robe, non doublée .
— *doublée* . 185 fr.

36925. **CLOCHE** en paille fantaisie blanche ou mordoré garnie roses roses .... **80** fr.

66946. **ROBE** en marocain coton, broderie blanche coloris du 66944. *La robe* .... **79** fr.
En serge coloris du 66944 broderie couleur assortie. *La robe* ...... **115** fr.
En jersey laine uni, coloris du 66941 *Prix* .... **125** fr.
En marocain de laine, amande rouille **135** f.
castor, gris marine et noir. *La robe*.
36924. **Petit CHAPEAU** en laize de crin noir ou nègre, garniture assortie. **75** f.

66948 **ROBE** en popeline marine ou noire, broderie couleur ou assortie. *La robe* **145** fr.
En marocain de laine, coloris du 66946.
La robe ... **155** fr.
En crêpe marocain gros grain, acajou, castor, nègre, amande, gris, vieux bleu, marine ou noir. **195** fr.
36926. **Petit CHAPEAU** en laize brillante marron, garni gland effilé soie assorti .... **59** fr.

66947.
ROBE-MANTEAU en serge pure laine, marine ou noire broderie lacet . **210** fr.
En popeline belle qualité marine ou noire. **225** fr.
13927. **CAPELINE** en crêpe de Chine noir, calotte en tagal, garnie motif de perles, tons écossais, 95 fr.

66949 **ROBE** en crêpe de Chine, nœud de même tissu avec boucle, mêmes coloris que le 66 942. **150** fr.
En marocain gros grain, coloris du 66948.
La robe .. **175** fr.
En marocain gros grain, fond amande, de, rouille, bleu, noir imprimé couleur, fond blanc imprimé noir. *La robe.*
36928. **PETITE CLOC** satin noir garni broder paille cerise ....

Pour nous permettre de répondre mieux et plus rapidement aux désirs de notre Clientèle, nous la prions de bien vouloir se con mer autant que possible aux prescriptions indiquées aux pages suivantes.

Robes

Au Printemps
paris

66952.
E en voile de
broderie blanche,
du 66942.
robe
oublée ... **99** fr.
...... **115** fr.
arocain de soie,
mordoré, marine
re, brodé ton sur
La robe **145** fr.
me, entièrement
ain imprimé, colo-
66949.
...... **125** fr.

66950.
ROBE en crêpe marocain
coton, coloris du 66944,
brodé blanc. *La robe*
125 fr

En crêpe de Chine marine,
mordoré, noir, amande,
brodée ton sur ton, en
mauve, corail, jade. blanc.
brodée blanc. *La role* **235** fr.

66951.
ROBE en ma-
rocain coton,
broderie blan-
che, coloris du
66944. *La robe*
99 fr

En serge marine ou noire,
broderie rouille, vieux
bleu ou assortie. *La*
robe .... **150** fr.
En marocain gros grain,
nègre, écaille, marine,
gris ou noir, brodée ton
sur ton. *La robe* **195** fr.

66953.
ROBE en voile
de coton, pan-
neaux plissés,
fine broderie
blanche, coloris
du 66942.
La robe
non doublée
135 fr.
Doublée. **150** fr.

En voile de laine, marine,
noir, beige, vieux-bleu
et gris brodée ton sur
ton. *La robe doublée*
soyeux assorti .. **250** fr.
En crêpe de Chine coloris
du 66942, broderie assor-
tie .... *La robe* **295** fr.

66954.
ROBE en
marocain gros
grain imprimé de plusieurs
tons, jolie boucle. **160** fr.
La robe ....
En crêpe de Chine, coloris
du 66942. *La robe*.. **150** fr.
En crêpe marocain gros
grain, coloris du 66948.
La robe .... **185** fr.

N'OUBLIEZ PAS DE NOUS INDIQUER : LA TEINTE

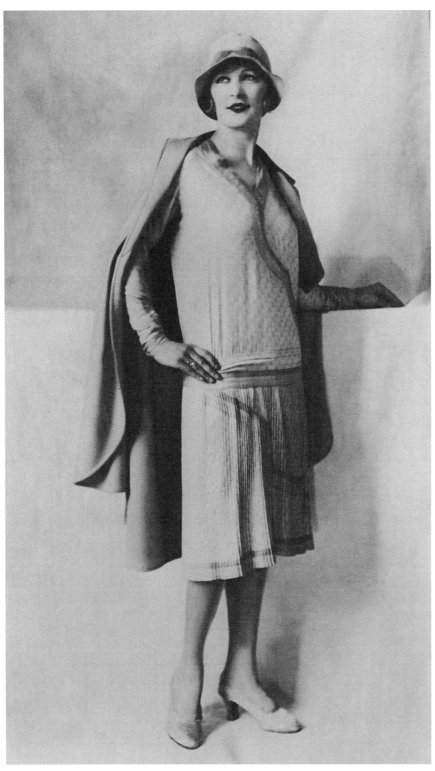

Left and right
A Parisian ensemble, c.1924. The model
wears a beige cape draped off the
shoulders with a light silk dress that has a
knife-pleated skirt in beige and red.

Four spring dresses for young women.
Paris Mode, c.1924

7306

7307

7308

7309

Paris-Mode

29, Rue de la Sourdière
PARIS (1er arrt)

Les fraiches toilettes juvéniles

SUPPLÉMENT
N° 227   Pl. 477

Right and opposite
A transparent embroidered gold brocade
dress worn over a black crêpe slip,
accessorized with a large crinoline hat
trimmed with a large fabric rose, c.1924

A Parisian model in red and white
printed crêpe, with long sleeves
and jabot flounces, c.1924

Daywear

Right
Studio fashion photograph of the
'Canada' creation by Groult, c.1925.
The design on the dress is described
as 'Indian', which in this instance
refers to Canadian First Nations and
it incorporates stylised traditional First
Nations' designs. This type of stylistic
appropriation is an example of less
obvious Orientalism in fashion.

877

Atelier Bachwitz

Left
Afternoon dress of black faille with
coloured velvet application bordered
with pleated silver galloons by Atelier
Bachroitz. *Chic Parisien Beaux-Arts
des Modes*, 1925

Above
Two-piece afternoon outfit of blue
and white crêpe de Chine, c.1925.
The jumper is elaborately encrusted with
tiny seed pearls in rich stylised wave
designs, while the loose fitting blue coat
is piped and embroidered to match the
jumper design. A tight-fitting cloche hat
completes the outfit. The wave design
is probably inspired by Katsushika
Hokusai's 'Great Wave off Kanagawa'
woodblock print from c.1829.

63

ALBUM TAILLEUR
DE LUXE

Above and right
Purple skirt suit, the jacket trimmed with
fur. *Album Tailleur de Luxe*, c.1925

A tiered afternoon summer day dress
worn with a straw hat and white gloves.
France, c.1925

Daywear

22

114

23

Above
A sleeveless walking ensemble in blue, white and red with a blue belt and tri-colour cloche hat. France, c.1925

Right
Postcard of a Marshall autumn model showing an embellished silk crêpe dress with sash-tie. USA, c.1925

Daywear

A
MARSHALL
AUTUMN
MODEL

Right
A long sleeved blue, white and red day
dress, accessorized with a large yellow
artificial flower on the shoulder, and
a blue cloche hat with smaller yellow
flowers. France, c.1925

No 328
„Chic Parisien"

Above and right
Silk velvet afternoon robe banded with
chinchilla fur and an afternoon velvet
dress with silk and gold embroidery by
Atelier Bachroitz. *Chic Parisien Beaux-
Arts des Modes*, 1925

Sweater frock of wool velour with ocelot
fur collar and cuffs by Atelier Bachroitz.
*Chic Parisien Beaux-Arts
des Modes*, 1925

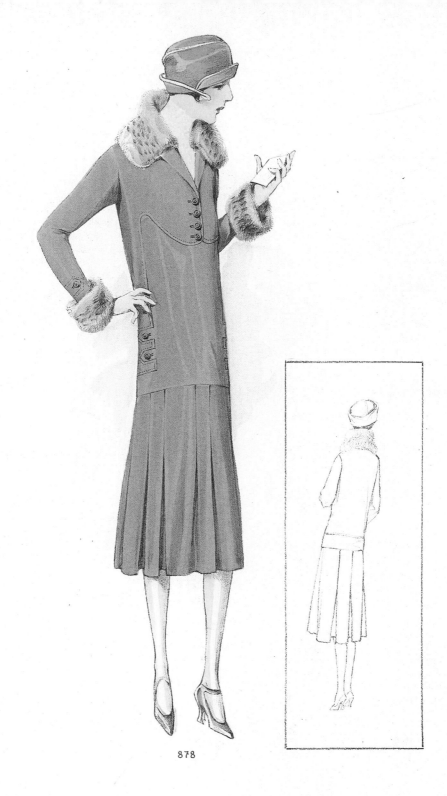

878

Atelier Bachwitz

Above
Four day dresses by Maison Gerda.
Maison Gerda catalogue, c.1925

Four day dresses by Maison Gerda.
Maison Gerda catalogue, c.1925

Daywear

La Femme Chic
SUPPLÉMENT
Nº 170.   Pl. 582.

QUELQUES BLOUSES SIMPLES

II. Création Redfern

Above and right
Designs for a coat and simple blouses,
including a checked design by Redfern.
La Femme Chic, c.1925

A two-piece black satin costume by
French designer Marthe Dion with a
jumper of white Georgette and satin
giving the effect of a waistcoat, c.1923

Daywear

N° 500   N" 501   N° 900   N° 502

Left
Five knitwear designs by Maison Gerda.
Maison Gerda catalogue, c.1925

N° 503   N° 504

Above left and right
Four day dresses by Maison Gerda.
Maison Gerda catalogue, c.1925

Four day dresses by Maison Gerda.
Maison Gerda catalogue, c.1925

Daywear

Right
Two walking outfits and an afternoon
dress. Au Louvre catalogue, 1925

Daywear

AU
LOUVRE
PARIS

ÉTÉ 1925

Left and above
Model posing in a white satin jumper
blouse with a *trompe l'oeil* pattern
by La Maison David, c.1925

Designs for blouses including
designs by Bernard and Lucien
Lelong. La *Femme Chic*, c.1925

336

887

888

Atelier Bachroitz

336   887   888

Above
An afternoon dress of crêpe satin with
bell pleats, a satin afternoon dress with
slashed front and bell shaped tunic, and
a satin princess robe with faille ribbon
cravats by Atelier Bachroitz. *Chic Parisien
Beaux-Arts des Modes*, 1925

Right
A rust-coloured afternoon dress with
tiered skirt panels accessorized with a
large fox fur stole. *Paris Élégant*, c.1925

Daywear

9265

9416

9417   9418

Above and right
Three sportswear style ensembles.
Paris Élégant, c.1925

Designs for blouses and sweaters.
La Femme Chic, c.1925

Daywear

136

Below
A knitted jumper and pleated
skirt ensemble, c.1926

Right
Designs for sports and city blouses
including two pink and black
embroidered designs by Lucien
Lelong. *La Femme Chic*, c.1925

La Femme Chic
SUPPLÉMENT

Nº 177.   Pl. 662.

BLOUSES DE SPORT ET DE VILLE

I. Création Lelong.

138

Left and opposite
Afternoon ensemble with pleated skirt and sleeves and a tasselled scarf blouse by Alice Bernard. *La Femme Chic*, 1926

Black and white checked dress with drop waist by Martial et Armand. *Le Style Parisien*, 1926

Modèle BERNARD et Cᵢᵉ,

Photo H. MANUEL,

Left
Actress Jacqueline Gadsden who
starred alongside Clara Bow in *It*,
modelling a morning dress of blue
flat crêpe trimmed with silver braid
that forms a vestee and is also used
to edge the patch pocket, c.1926

Above
Day dress with lace collar by Bernard et
Cie. *La Femme Elégant à Paris*, 1926

Daywear

Left

Two day dresses. *Sélection*, c.1927. The black dress is very similar to Coco Chanel's Little Black Dress of 1926.

Below

An in-between dress with a straight collar overlaid with lace and fancy openwork underlaid with coloured silk, a dress with Medici collar and box pleat skirt, and a street dress of plain silk with horizontal wool panels by Atelier Bachroitz. *Grande mode Parisienne*, 1926

1097   1098   1099   *Atelier Bachroitz*

Supplément au No. 315

Daywear

Sweater dress in Kasha with pleated skirt,
a spring dress with embroidered collar and
material straps trimmed with buttons, and
a cashmere sweater dress with an inverted
pleats skirt by Atelier Bachroitz. *Grande
mode Parisienne*, 1926

1103

1104

1105

Atelier Bachroitz

Supplément au No. 315

Sweater dress with silk belt and shoulder straps, a woollen dress with bolero gathered at the sides, and a silk sweater dress with a top of patterned silk and a plain silk skirt drawn in pleats at the side by Atelier Bachroitz. *Grande mode Parisienne*, 1926

Right
Bright pink walking dress with a run-through tie, a walking dress with narrow strap details of deer skin, and a crêpe sweater dress with cravat and pleated skirt by Atelier Bachroitz. *Grande mode Parisienne*, 1926

Right
Street dress with triangular pockets and embroidered belt, an ensemble in charmelaine with a bolero and ruches of crêpe, and a day dress with a straight collar, gathered skirt and a tight neck plastron by Atelier Bachroitz. *Grande mode Parisienne*, 1926

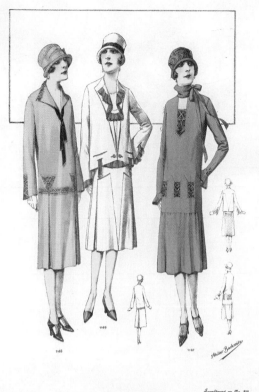

Left
Silk crêpe afternoon dress with lace jabot and sleeve ruches, an ensemble in plain and patterned silk with a short sleeved bolero, and a silk poplin afternoon dress with a pleated collar by Atelier Bachroitz. *Grande mode Parisienne*, 1926

Daywear

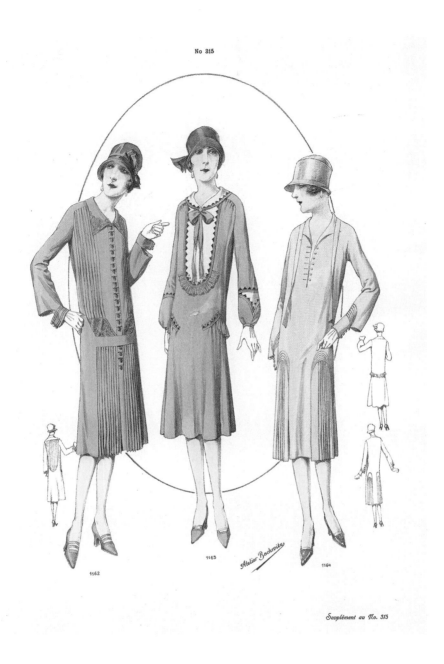

No 315

1162   1165   1164

Atelier Bachroitz

Supplément au No. 315

Above
Poplin dress with inserted pleated
panels, a silk princess robe with a
cravat, puffed sleeves and pleated
ruching, and a silk princess robe with
curved skirt panels drawn in opposite
pleats by Atelier Bachroitz. *Grande mode
Parisienne*, 1926

Next page
Six afternoon dresses
by Atelier Bachroitz. *Grande
mode Parisienne*, 1926

Daywear

1091

1092

1093

1094   1095

1096   *Atelier Bachwitz*

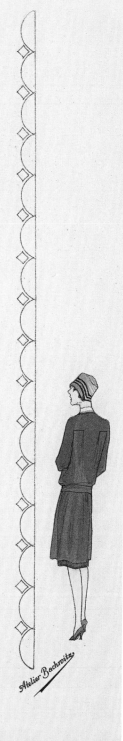

377

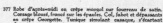

377 Robe d'après=midi en crêpe mongol sur fourreau de satin.
Corsage blousé, froncé sur les épaules. Col, jabot et dépassants
en crêpe Georgette. Tunique simulant casaque, s'écartant
devant.

Atelier Bachwitz

Modèles Originaux

352

Modèles Originaux

358

Left and right above
A coat dress in pale brown Kasha edged
in matching silk by Atelier Bachroitz,
Modèles Originaux, c.1926

A brown velvet dress with a square
neckline, ornamental stitching and
large buttons by Atelier Bachroitz,
Modèles Originaux, c.1926

Left
Blue tunic dress in Mongolian
crêpe with satin flounced collar
and cuffs by Atelier Bachroitz,
Modèles Originaux, c.1926

Daywear

Mars 1926   REVUE MENSUELLE   Le N° France : 7 francs. — Italie : Lire 1

La femme chic

à Paris

Alb. Jarach e P. Chambry

Telefono 85-855
La femme chic
DI A. PIERONI
GIORNALI DI MODE · MODELLI
TAGLIATI IN CARTA E MUSSOLA
MANNEQUINS MILANO VIA DANTE, 4

A. LOUCHEL, Éditeur

NUMÉRO SPÉCIAL DES MODES DE PRINTEMPS

La Femme Chic   LES SWEATERS EN VOGUE

Left and above
Cover of *La Femme Chic à Paris*,
March 1926

Four 'fashionable' sweaters.
La Femme Chic 1926

Daywear

Right
Four long blouses. *La Femme Chic*, 1926

156

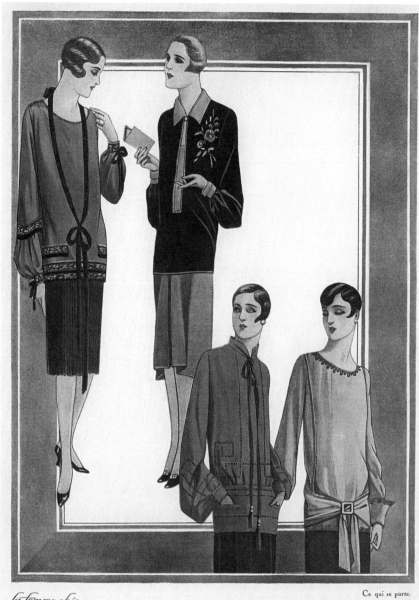

La Femme Chic
SUPPLÉMENT · Nº 192. Pl. 187.

Ce qui se porte.

Above
Designs for four blouses.
La Femme Chic, c.1926

Daywear

'Le Chic du Noir' (stylish black) dress with a flounced lace collar and cuffs by Magdeleine des Hayes, *La Femme Chic*, 1926

Right
Several dresses for the spring
by Magdeleine des Hayes.
La Femme Chic, 1926

Left
Black pleated afternoon dress.
La Femme Chic, 1926

Above
Afternoon dress with flaring
pleated sleeves by Alice Bernard.
La Femme Chic, 1926

Modèles Originaux

368

368 Robe en crêpe de Chine et velours façonné. Ceinture et écharpe même tissu. Jupe à larges plis couchés incrustés sur les deux côtés.

Atelier Bachroitz

Above
Beige day dress in crêpe de Chine and jacquard velvet with pleated side panels and a matching scarf by Atelier Bachroitz, *Modèles Originaux* c.1926

Right
Day dress in brown patterned velvet by Atelier Bachroitz, *Modèles Originaux*, c.1926

331

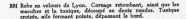

331 Robe en velours de Lyon. Corsage retombant, ainsi que les manches et la tunique, découpé en dents rondes. Tunique croisée, aile formant pointe, dépassant le bord.

Atelier Bachroitz

164

Above left and right
Petrol blue afternoon dress in shiny satin
with a v-neckline and a petalled skirt
by Atelier Bachroitz *Modèles Originaux*,
c.1926

Blue day dress in ribbed crêpe with
diagonal panels for the skirt by Atelier
Bachroitz *Modèles Originaux*, c.1926

Daywear

165

Above left and right
Four 'sportswear' blouses by Dupony.
La Femme Chic, 1926

Four 'sportswear' blouses.
La Femme Chic, 1926

Daywear

Right
Cover of *La Femme Chic*, April 1926

Avril 1926   REVUE MENSUELLE   Le N° France : 6 francs. — Italie : Lire 9.

La femme chic

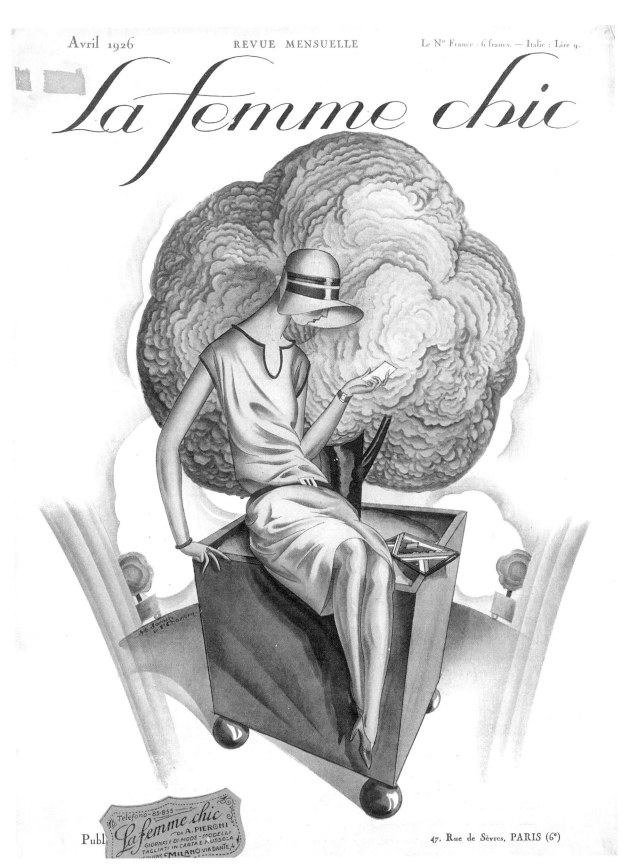

Telefono 85-855

La femme chic
DI A. PIERONI
GIORNALI DI MODE - MODELLI
TAGLIATI IN CARTA E PI USSOLA
MILANO VIA DANTE, 4

Publ

47, Rue de Sèvres, PARIS (6e)

Below and right
Afternoon dress with large buckle
and trumpet sleeves by Alice Bernard.
La Femme Chic, 1926

Simple blouses and a velour sweater,
La Femme Chic, 1926

Right
'For the Easter Vacation', grey ensemble by Alice Bernard, red ensemble with oriental motifs by Lina Mouton, turquoise ensemble and black tunic dress by Alice Bernard, floral patterned dress with flounced tiered skirt, pink dress with lace panels and collar by Francis, and dress made from 'Les Fleurs de Thuya' fabric by Francis. *La Femme Chic*, 1926

1244.

1245.

1246.

1247.

1248.

1249.

Above
Selection of day dresses.
La Femme Élégante à Paris, 1926

1250.

1251.

1252.

1253.

1254.

1255.

Above
Selection of day dresses.
La Femme Élégante à Paris, 1926

Daywear

Above
Two travelling dresses by Zimmermann.
La Femme Chic, 1926

Travelling dress by Bernard and lilac
travelling dress by Zimmermann. *La
Femme Chic*, 1926

2016 Robe de thé en Crêpe de Chine. Col noué. Plastron plissé et bouffants des manches de crêpe Georgette Motifs perlés. Ceinture de tissu avec boucle émail.

2017 Robe pour le bridge en crêpe satin. Petit plastron, bandes et godets incrustés du côté brillant du tissu. Ceinture nouée à droite.

Atelier Bachroitz

Above
Crêpe afternoon dress with front tie collar, and a crêpe bridge dress with circular bands on the bodice and sleeves by Atelier Bachroitz. *Chic Parisien Beaux-Arts des Modes*, 1927

Left
Two outfits for country receptions by Paul Poiret. *La Femme Chic*, 1927

Previous page and above
Five afternoon dresses.
Fashion for All, 1927

Three skirt suits with matching
cloche hats. *Sélection*, c.1927

Right
Two day coats accessorized with tight
fitting cloche hats. *Sélection*, c.1927

Below
A beach dress in cream washed silk
with a pleated skirt and a openwork lace
detailed blouse-style top, 1927

2018

2019

2018

2019

2018 Robe d'après-midi en velours chiffon. Echancrure carrée, traversée par une cravate de tissu. Nervures à droite et aux manches. Jupe formée de deux volants en forme. Ceinture avec boucle bijouterie.

2019 Robe de visite en marocain. Bandes de tissu formant dents dans le dos, croisées devant de genre fichu. Bandes de ceinture incrustées. Petits drapés fixés par des boucles acier.

Atelier Bachroitz

Above
Chiffon velvet afternoon dress, and
a silk afternoon dress with draped panels
fixed with buckles by Atelier Bachroitz.
*Chic Parisien Beaux-Arts
des Modes*, 1927

Daywear

2020 Robe princesse en crêpe satin. Echancrure carrée dans le dos, en cœur devant et terminée par une boucle bijouterie. Lé de côté formant pan et drapé par une boucle pareille. Incrustations disposées en biais du côté brillant du tissu.

2021 Robe de thé en satin. Boléro brodé soie de couleur et métal, petits boutons de métal. Col avec cravate. Volants de jupe divisés à droite. Ceinture écharpe de tissu avec long pan.

Atelier Bachroitz

Above
Crêpe satin princess dress with two jeweled buckles, and a satin afternoon dress with a metal and silk bolero jacket and cravat collar by Atelier Bachroitz.
Chic Parisien Beaux-Arts des Modes, 1927

2000 Toilette de thé en crêpe de Chine clair. Longue casaque. Broderie anglaise sont cernée de perles. Manches garnies de séries de perles. Poignets et bordure de renard. Fourreau de mousseline bordé de satin foncé.

2001 Toilette d'après-midi en crêpe satin. Haut croisé. Incrustation et volant en forme du côté brillant du tissu. Manches pareilles rapportées en dent. Ceinture de tissu.

Atelier Bachroitz

Right
Crêpe de Chine afternoon dress with a tunic decorated with hole embroidery and trimmed with beads over a chiffon slip hemmed with satin, and an afternoon dress of crêpe band laid diagonally by Atelier Bachroitz. *Chic Parisien Beaux-Arts des Modes*, 1927

186

2004 Robe de thé .en crêpe satin. Corsage croisé avec jabot drapé du côté
gauche, fixé par des pierres de verre de couleur. Boucle de ceinture assortie.
Bandes incrustées et lés du dos du côté brillant du tissu.

2005 Robe d'après-midi en faille. Revers d'un côté et dépassant de jupe en crêpe
mat. Rose de métal à l'épaule gauche. Lé flottant fixé par une boucle
de perles.

Atelier Bachroitz

Above

Crêpe satin afternoon dress with a
crossed waist and draped left panel kept
in place with a large brooch, and an
afternoon dress of faille with a crossed
waist and a flaring underskirt kept in
place with a large bead buckle by Atelier
Bachroitz. *Chic Parisien Beaux-Arts des
Modes*, 1927

Right

Black dress in crêpe de Chine with
a full length flounce and a silk rose
by Premet. *La Femme Chic*, 1927

Daywear

Right
Velvet afternoon dress with scalloped
tiering, and a faille afternoon dress with
a slashed bolero top and two bell-shaped
skirt flounces by Atelier Bachroitz. *Chic
Parisien Beaux-Arts des Modes*, 1927

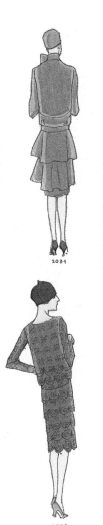

2031

2030

2030

2031

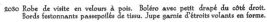

Atelier Bachwitz

2030 Robe de visite en velours à pois. Boléro avec petit drapé du côté droit.
Bords festonnants passepoilés de tissu. Jupe garnie d'étroits volants en forme.

2031 Robe de thé en faille. Boléro ouvert des deux côtés. Echarpe nouée avec
long pan flottant. Ceinture de tissu avec boucle perlée. Jupe à deux
volants en forme.

Daywear

Above
Evening dress and skirt suit
with tuxedo-style jacket.
Fashion for All, 1927

Right
Satin crêpe afternoon dress with
diagonal bands, and an afternoon
dress of Georgette trimmed with silk lace
by Atelier Bachroitz. *Chic Parisien Beaux-
Arts des Modes*, 1927

2008

2009

2008

2009

2008 Robe d'après-midi en crêpe satin. Tunique appliquée, formant pans. Bandes et nœud dans le dos du côté brillant du tissu.

2009 Robe de visite en crêpe Georgette garnie de dentelle soie. Nids d'abeilles aux épaules. Empiècement rond, noué dans le dos, avec pan flottant. Ceinture écharpe de tissu.

Atelier Bachwitz

Above left and right
Black day dress in chiffon velvet with
old gold embroidered motifs, draped at
the front and terminating in points and
accessorized with a lamé scarf by Atelier
Bachroitz, *Modèles Originaux*, c.1927

Velvet afternoon dress with silver lace
and burgundy velvet panels gathered at
the back and with a crossover flounce
at the front by Atelier Bachroitz, *Modèles
Originaux*, c.1927

Daywear

Above
Three blouses with stylised floral and
geometric motifs. *La Femme Chic*, 1927

Above and right
Two day suits by Martial et Armand
and a grey checked suit by Paul Poiret.
Le Femme Chic, 1927

Two day dresses with side and back
flounces and panels by Atelier Bachroitz.
Chic Parisien, Beaux-Arts des Modes,
c.1928

Next page
'Light dresses for Spa Towns', pink and
black dress, red dress and blue and lilac
dress with sprig motif by Zimmermann;
navy dress and beige dress by Premet;
dress with 'Le Tourbillon de fleurs
champêtres' fabric; 'sports' dress in
'Djersa Kasha' fabric by Zimmermann.
La Femme Chic, 1927

„Chic Parisien"

2855

2856

Atelier Bachwitz

Daywear

Left and above
Actress Kathryn Crawford in a blue
and white plaid taffeta and navy blue
Georgette crêpe ensemble with an
accordion pleated skirt and tight bodice,
1928

Actress Dorothy Gulliver in a white silk
mull afternoon dress trimmed with lace,
and a sash of rose-coloured ribbon is
fastened at the side of the waist with long
loops hanging almost to the floor, 1928

Daywear

Right
Mademoiselle Chanel in Biarritz,
France, 1928

1920s Outerwear

Above
Two tailored suits by Doeuillet.
L'Illustration des Modes, 1920

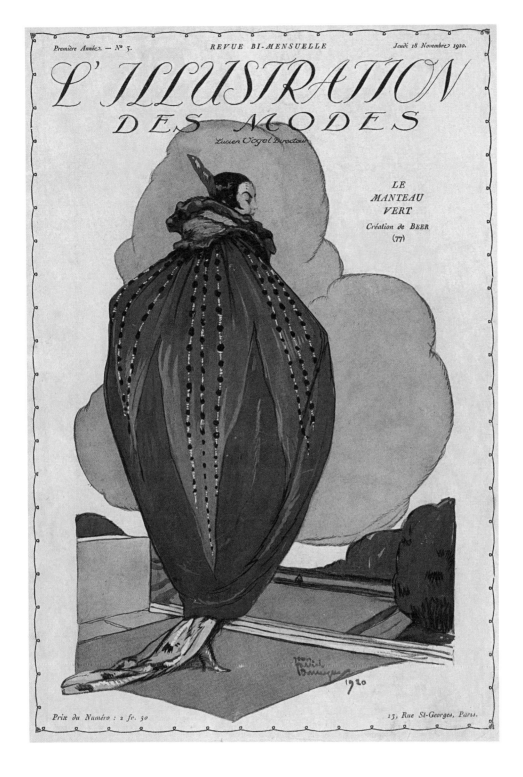

Green evening coat by Beer.
L'Illustration des Modes, 1920

Above

'Au Polo' (At Polo) – grey woollen coat by Paquin, brown tailored ensemble by Worth, red and blue skirt suit by Jenny, beige and brown tailored ensemble by Beer, black ensemble with green vest by Lanvin, and brown jacket and skirt with Morrocan-style motif by Poiret. *L'Illustration des Modes*, 1920

Left and above
'Sommes-nous les dernières?'
(Are we the last?) – two ensembles in
velour with chenille belts by Redfern.
L'Illustration des Modes, 1920

'Appelez Urbain de L'avenue du Bois',
evening coat by Beer. Illustration
By Pierre Brissaud. *Gazette du Bon
Ton*, 1920

Outerwear

1. MANTEAU en drap, droit et ample dans le bas, dont un des côtés croise sur l'autre. Des bandes de plis plats sont rapportées au col, aux manches et sur deux rangs, ainsi que sur les hanches où elles s'évasent en poches.

Métrage: 4 mètres en 1 m. 40.

2. TAILLEUR fantaisie en serge. Petite veste à panneaux froncés sur les hanches. Col droit et emmanchures basses. Étroite ceinture de daim à la taille et jolie broderie en raphia. La jupe est tout unie dans le haut, mais brodée dans le bas.

Métrage: 5 m. 50 en 1 m. 20.

3. ÉLÉGANTE ROBE de taffetas, dont l'ample jupe froncée autour des hanches se pose sur un fond plus étroit. Corsage plat, légèrement drapé, avec ou sans nœud dans le dos; il est brodé, ainsi que la jupe, d'arabesques au point de chaînette.

Métrage: 5 mètres en 0 m. 70.

4. ROBE de foulard uni et foulard imprimé. La partie unie forme le dos du costume qui boutonne dans le dos. Le devant, ainsi que le bas des manches, sont à grands dessins.

Métrage: 5 mètres en 0 m. 50.

Prix de chaque patron, 42, 44, 46, franco : 3 fr. 50.

Above
'J'ai le bout du nez Rouge ou Un
malheur vite repare' (The tip of
my nose is red or an easily fixed
misfortune), winter ensemble by Worth.
Illustration By André Edouard Marty.
Gazette du Bon Ton, 1920

Right
Three walking dresses with waist
sashes. *Les Dernières Modes de
Paris*, 1920

1. ROBE en fine serge. Le blouson du corsage et la jupe sont brodés de pastilles au point de chaînette d'un ton différent. Col et gilet blancs. Les côtés de la jupe froncés et drapés s'évasent légèrement.

Métrage: 3 mètres serge en 1 m. 30; 0 m. 40 tissu blanc pour le gilet.

2. ROBE simple s'ouvrant sur un gilet plat. Les côtés du corsage sont agrémentés de boutonnières. Un grand col-pèlerine recouvre entièrement les épaules. Large ceinture drapée, retournée en écharpe et frangée au bord. Les panneaux de la jupe sont brodés et laissent voir des crevés de drap gris clair sur les côtés.

Métrage: 3 m. 50 tissu en 1 m. 30; 0 m. 40 tissu clair pour le gilet et les crevés.

3. ROBE en voile et serge. Le corsage en serge descend un peu au-dessous de la taille et supporte la tunique plissée en voile assorti. Biais de voile autour des panneaux du corsage, du col et des poignets. Ceinture de velours serrant à peine la taille.

Métrage: 3 mètres serge en 1 m. 30; 3 mètres voile en 1 m. 10.

1. MANTEAU en djersabure droit devant. Le col, très évasé, est entièrement brodé ; la même garniture agrémente le bas des manches et les côtés de la ceinture. Basque rapportée et froncée autour de la taille.

Métrage: 5 m. 50 tissu en 1 m. 30.

2. ROBE en faille gauloise. Le corsage croisé se noue de côté et s'ouvre sur un gilet matelassé, ainsi que le bas de la tunique. La manche est gracieusement découpée au coude et serrée autour du poignet.

Métrage: 4 mètres tissu en 1 m. 30.

3. COSTUME fanta'sie en diaffine. La veste dro te s'ouvre sur un g let à carreaux posé en bia s, ainsi que le col, les parements et les poches. Jupe composée de deux panneaux détachés laissant voir une quille de tissu écossais ourlé de tissu uni.

Métrage: 3 m.tres tissu uni ; 1 m. 35 tissu écossais.

Above
Three walking outfits.
Les Dernières Modes de Paris, 1920

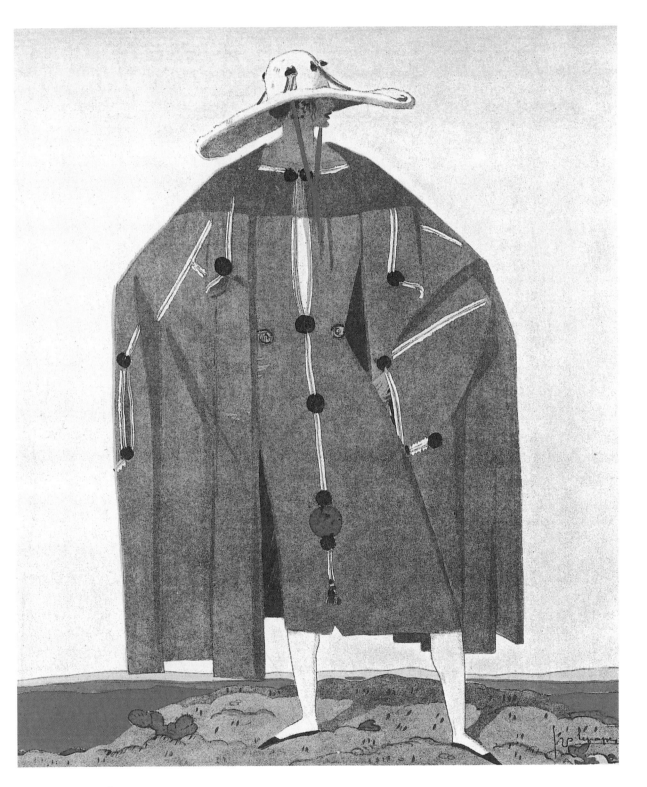

Above
'Tanger ou Les charmes de l'exil'
(Tangiers or the charm of being in exile),
afternoon dress and cape by Paul Poiret.
Illustration by George Lepape. *Gazette
du Bon Ton*, 1920

Left and above
'Gros temps' (Stormy weather), yachting
outfit. *Gazette du Bon Ton*, 1920

A woman in a red cape coat
trimmed with white fur. The red
boots are protected with snow
shoes. *La Mode*, 1920

Outerwear

Left
Grey cape with fur trim by Chéruit,
brown coat with V-shape back by
Worth, and black buttoned cape by
Lanvin, Illustration by Pierre Brissaud,
L'Illustration des Modes, 1920

Below
'A las Baleares' (To the Balearics),
skirt suit by Beer. Illustration by
Benito. *Gazette du Bon Ton*, 1921

A LAS
BALEARES

COSTUME TAILLEUR, DE BEER   Nº 6 de la Gazette du Bon Ton. Année 1921. — Planche 48

Below
Four coat models for spring.
La Nouveauté Française, 1921

La Nouveauté Française

Right
Grey and black silk walking dress
and blue coat suit with sheepskin
fur trim, hat and muffler. *Journal des
Demoiselles*, 1921

Extrait des « Élégances Parisiennes »

A. THIÉRY, DIRECTEUR
79, Boulev. Saint-Germain, PARIS

Bleuet
PARIS
364

Left and above
A French postcard featuring a model
in a hieroglyph design coat, 1923.
Egyptian motifs became immensely
popular in fashion after Howard
Carter's discovery of Tutankhamen's
tomb in 1922.

Two cape and dress designs by Paul
Carat. *The Delineator*, 1922

Right
Postcard of a model in a brown day
suit and patterned blouse with a
matching cloche hat, 1922

P.C
PARIS
827

wjaar

Right
Four luxurious fur or
fur-trimmed coats, c.1922

230

Above and right
Four fur-trimmed coats. *Le Chic
et la Mode*, c.1923

Four afternoon coats with wide
collars. *Le Chic et la Mode*, 1923

Outerwear

MANTEAUX J'APRES MIDI

1076

1075

1074

1077

fev.23

Le Chic et la Mode

La Femme Chic
SUPPLÉMENT
Nº 115.   Pl. 924.

TROIS TAILLEURS NOUVEAUX

1. Tailleur élégant en "Cottaline"
gris souris et satin noir.

Left and above
Three elegant skirt suits.
La Femme Chic, c.1923

Mouse grey 'cottaline' and black
satin skirt suit and two other tailored
skirt suits. *La Femme Chic*, c.1923

Outerwear

Below
Three suits and jackets. *La Femme Chic*, c.1923. All the coats are trimmed with fur showing a Russian influence.

Right
Black and white costume over a straight crêpe dress, c.1923. The black satin coat is lined with white satin and boasts a circular hem, while the hat is adorned with long drooping feathers.

La Femme Chic
SUPPLÉMENT
Nº 131.   Pl. 151.

TROIS TAILLEURS PRIS AUX COURSES

III. Costume en "Kashadrap".

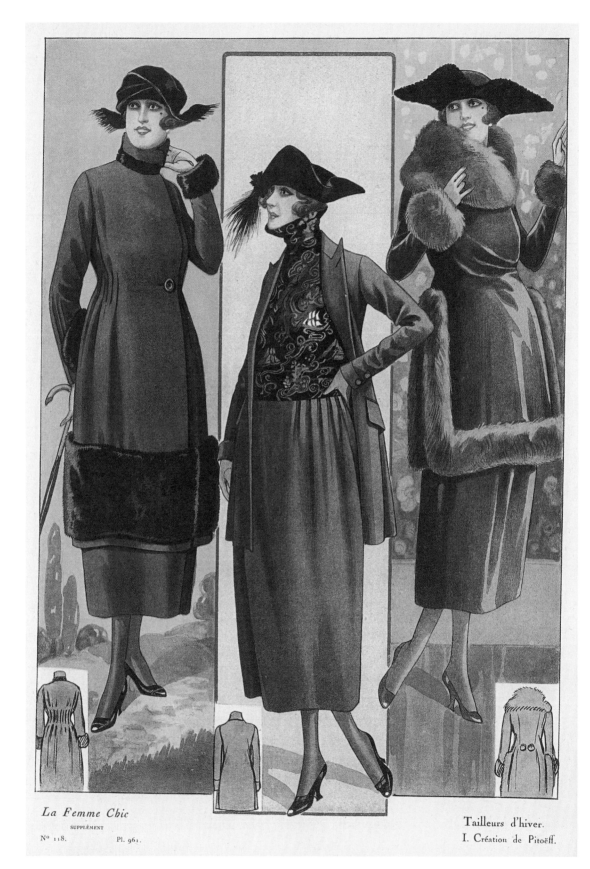

La Femme Chic

SUPPLÉMENT

Nº 118.   Pl. 961.

Tailleurs d'hiver.

I. Création de Pitoëff.

Left and right
Three winter suits.
La Femme Chic, c.1923

A gold and silver brocade and
black lace evening cape. *Dernières
Creations*, c.1923

Below left and right
Selection of day coats,
Printemps catalogue, 1924

Selection of knitted suits,
Printemps catalogue, 1924

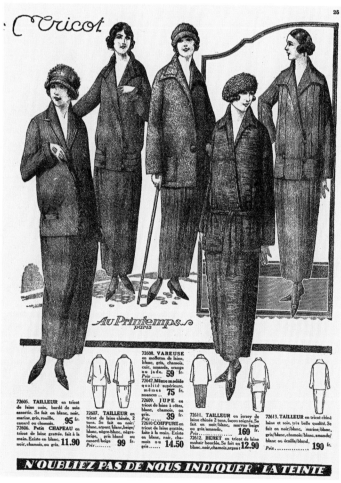

Below left and right
Selection of day and evening coats
and capes, Printemps catalogue, 1924

Selection of skirt suits,
Printemps catalogue, 1924

240

Au Printemps paris

Ne pas oublier de nous indiquer sur votre commande, la taille et la teinte du vêtement choisi.

N'OUBLIEZ PAS DE NOUS INDIQUER : LA TAILLE

Above
Selection of evening coats and jackets,
Printemps catalogue, 1924

Outerwear

Ne pas oublier sur votre commande de nous indiquer la taille et la teinte du vêtement choisi.

Au Printemps
paris

20134. Elégant MANTEAU 3/4, dernière nouveauté, en beau crêpe marocain noir, garni de petits volants superposés, entièrement doublé crêpe de Chine. Longueur 1m,05.
Prix............ **395** fr

20135. Le même, en beau satin soie noire.
Prix............ **425** fr.

20136. ROBE-MANTEAU en crêpe marocain noir, brodé amadou, argent ou noir, ou marocain nègre, brodé camaïeu, col et parements garnis bouillonnés, entièrement doublé crêpe de Chine. Longueur 1m,25.... **595** fr.

20137. Le même, en beau satin noir, brodé amadou, argent ou noir................ **600** fr.

20138. MANTEAU-ROBE en crêpe marocain soie noire 0; nègre, devants col et parements garnis volants superposés, entièrement doublé crêpe de Chine. Long. 1m,25. **435** fr.

20139. Le même, en beau crêpe marocain de laine, gris nouveau, tabac ou noir, 1/2 doublé soie. **275** fr.

20140. MANTEAU-ROBE, dernier genre, en beau crêpe marocain et satin soie noire, bandes interposées, entièrement doublé soie. **395** fr.

20141. Joli MANTEAU d'après-midi, en belle soie façonnée, noire ou nègre, col et parements garnis de bouillonné nouveaux, entièrement doublé crêpe de Chine. Long. 1m,25. **425** fr.
Prix........

20142. Le même, en crêpe marocain ou satin noir. **395** fr.

Nota. — Ces vêtements étant faits sur taille régulière de mannequins, nous prions nos clientes de bien vouloir nous indiquer la taille qu'elles désirent en se conformant au tableau ci-contre : Le 40 a 67 de taille et 90 de poitrine. | Le 42 a 69 de taille et 95 de poitrine. | Le 46 a 76 de taille et 105 de poitrine. | Le 50 a 83 de taille et 112 de poitrine. Le 44 a 73 — 100 — | Le 48 a 80 — 108 — | Le 52 a 86 — 115 —

Above
Selection of evening coats,
Printemps catalogue, 1924

242

Above
Three spring suits. The landscaped
gardens lend the outfits an air of high
class and sophistication. *La Femme Chic*,
c.1924

Right
Three coats and a cape by Atelier
Bachovitz, c.1924

Outerwear

135

136   137

134   135   136   137

Atelier Bachroitz

Below and right
Purple coat with ornamental stitching
and trimmed in fur. *Album Tailleur de
Luxe*, c.1925

Two models in fur coats, the left is made
of lambskin, while the right is made of
dyed rabbit-skin, c.1924

Previous page
Photograph of a fashion display in
a Parisian Couture salon, c.1924

ALBUM TAILLEUR
DE LUXE

Right
Four city coats by Maison
Gerda. Maison Gerda
catalogue, c.1925

70

ALBUM TAILLEUR
DE LUXE

Left
Autumn ensemble of a two-tone
brown coat, skirt and jacket
accessorized with a checked scarf.
Album Tailleur de Luxe, c.1925

Below
Three winter day suits described
as 'comfortable models'.
La Femme Chic, c.1925

Right
Hollywood actress Mae Bush wearing
a suit of Mesange blue Kasha
combined with the same shade of
crêpe de Chine. The coat is trimmed
with silver fox and the dress is made
with an uneven skirt. The hat is flesh-
coloured horse hair trimmed with a
pearl ornament and blue ribbon. This
press photograph announces that
Miss Mae will be wearing this outfit in
her upcoming Metro-Goldwyn-Mayer
production *Time, The Comedian*. The
outfit is attributed to Erté. 1925

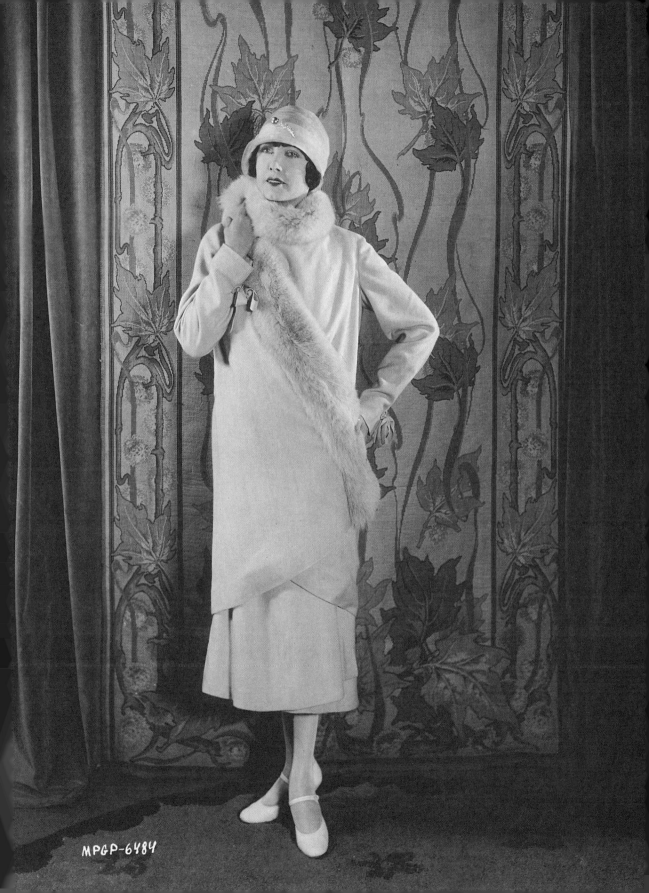

MPGP-6484

Above and right
Fall suit of flat 'American broadtail'
fur with a matching hat and handbag,
c.1925.

Winter ensemble of a grey and black
dress with elaborate red and silver
embroidery, and a black cape coat with
matching embroidery and trimmed in
grey fur. *Album Tailleur de Luxe*, c.1925

ALBUM TAILLEUR
DE LUXE

Above
A black velour winter coat trimmed
with fur, which instead of doing up is
supposed to be held together by the
wearer, c.1925

Above left and right
Street robe cut in scallops at the front
with pale fur collar and cuffs by Atelier
Bachroitz, *Chic Parisien Beaux-Arts
des Modes*, 1925

Velvet street dress with tight sleeves
and wide cuffs by Atelier Bachroitz –
both scarf and cuffs are embroidered
in wool. *Chic Parisien Beaux-Arts des
Modes*, 1925

Outerwear

881

882

Atelier Bachroitz

881

882

Above
An ensemble costume of Kasha and silk
crêpe with metal embroidered belt motif,
a full length coat with fur collar and cuffs,
an ensemble costume of checked wool
faced with silk crêpe and a wool velour
coat with fur collar, cuffs and banding
by Atelier Bachroitz. *Chic Parisien Beaux-
Arts des Modes*, 1925

Above and right
Three walking ensembles by Mariette
Pognot and the Welly Soeurs. *Paris
Élégante*, c.1925

A day dress with a pleated skirt and
matching skirt borders, waist panels
and cravat, and a dark orange coat
with a fur trim cuff and collar by
Mariette Pognot. *Paris Élégante*,
c.1925

Above
A day dress with a pleated skirt and
matching skirt borders, waist panels
and cravat, and a dark orange coat
with a fur trim cuff and collar by
Mariette Pognot. *Paris Élégante*,
c.1925

ALBUM TAILLEUR
DE LUXE

65

ALBUM TAILLEUR
DE LUXE

64

Above left to right

Purple ribbed velvet coat trimmed with
fur. *Album Tailleur de Luxe*, c.1925

Purple patterned velvet coat trimmed
with fur. *Album Tailleur de Luxe*,
c.1925

Outerwear

ALBUM TAILLEUR
DE LUXE

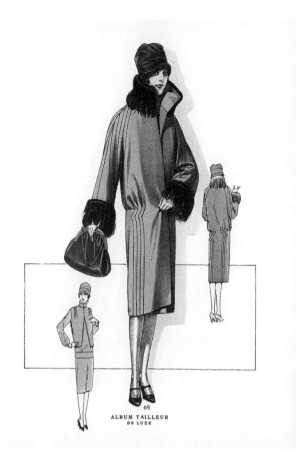

ALBUM TAILLEUR
DE LUXE

Above left and right
Single-breasted dark brown autumn coat
worn with a fur stole. *Album Tailleur de
Luxe*, c. 1925

Dark grey winter coat with ornamental
stitching and trimmed with black monkey
fur. *Album Tailleur de Luxe*, c.1925

Right
A dark green coat with pleated side
panels and trimmed with moleskin fur.
Album Tailleur de Luxe, c.1925

72

ALBUM TAILLEUR
DE LUXE

MANTEAUX
POUR
DAMES

22.110.

22.108.

22.107.

22.103.

22.106.

22.111.

22.104.

22.110.
Joli MANTEAU
crêpe soie noir ou
nègre, garni riche
broderie assortie,
entièrement doublé
soie.

Longueur 1m20.

385.»

22.108.
MANTEAU
rayures
nouveauté,
ottoman et
satin noir
travaillées en bandes, col
garni singe, entièrement
doublé soie.

Longueur 1m20.

425.»

22.107.
PALETOT
entièrement brodé,
dessin nouveau. Se
fait en marine et
argent, rouille et
vert, marron et
beige, noir et gris
et tout noir.

Longueur 0m80.

159.»

22.103.
MANTEAU
satin noir, garni broderie
nouveauté noir, ou noir
et or. Longueur 1m20.

195.»

Le même en satin
fulgurant, très belle
qualité.

250.»

22.111.
Élégant MANTEAU
crêpe satin noir belle qualité,
garni broderie or ou noir,
entièrement doublé soie.

Longueur 1m20.

475.»

22.106. CAPE
satin noir ou nègre, garnie belle
broderie, doublée crêpe de Chine.
Longueur 1m15.

425.»

La même, sans broderie.

22.104. MANTEAU
côtelé noir, nouveauté, entièrement
doublé soie.   Longueur 1m20.

295.»

En ottoman scintillant noir, qualité
extra.

Left and above
Selection of day and evening coats
and capes. Au Louvre catalogue, 1925

Wrap dress by Alice Bernard, a striped
summer suit in 'Pékins Buranic' fabric,
and a coral summer suit by Francis.
La Femme Chic, 1926

La Femme Chic
Supplément
N° 181.   Pl. 18.

QUELQUES TAILLEURS POUR LE MIDI

I. Costume en "Kasha"

La femme chic
Supplément « N° 190. Pl. 133.

I. Création Francis, Man-
teau   en   " Crêpelliver "
II. Création Alice Bernard.

Above left and right
Two day ensembles and a Kasha
ensemble trimmed with fur. *La Femme
Chic*, 1926

Coat and matching hat in 'Crêpelliver'
by Francis and two skirt suits by Alice
Bernard. *La Femme Chic*, 1926

Above
Two summer ensembles by Bernard
and an ensemble in checked Kasha.
La Femme Chic, 1926

268

Above and right
Driving ensemble in 'Diafil Crauté'.
La Femme Chic, 1926

Various designs for skirts.
La Femme Élégante à Paris, 1926

Outerwear

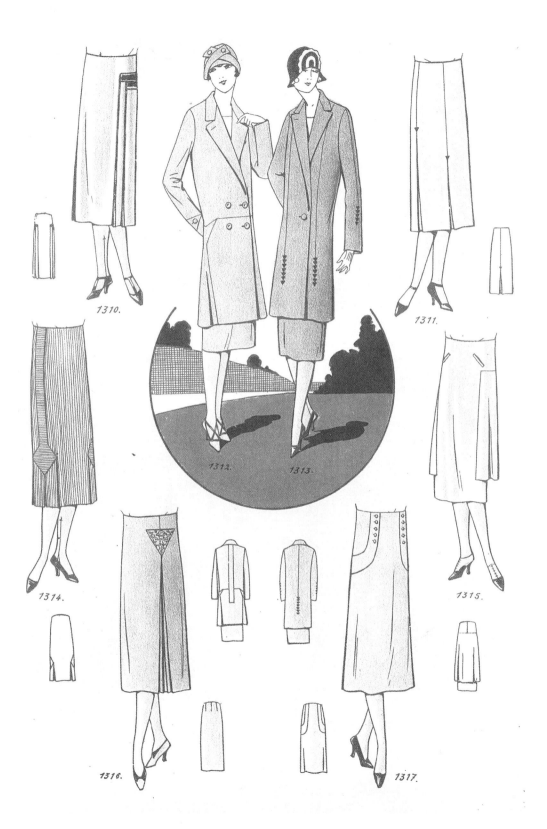

1310.

1311.

1312.

1313.

1314.

1315.

1316.

1317.

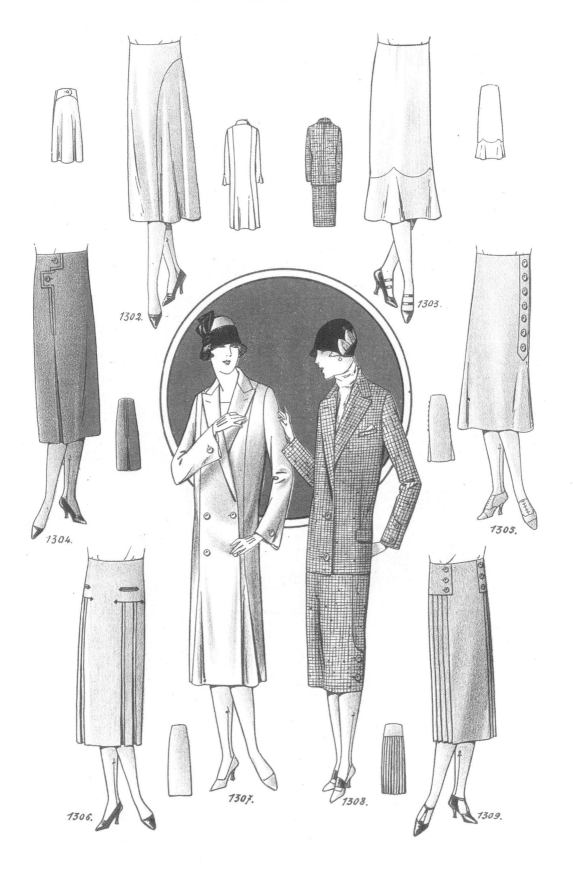

1302.

1303.

1304.

1305.

1306.

1307.

1308.

1309.

1280   1281

Above and left
Two designs for skirt suits.
La Femme Élégante à Paris, 1926

Various designs for skirts.
La Femme Élégante à Paris, 1926

1276   1277

Above
Two designs for skirt suits. The right-
hand model is a tuxedo suit worn
with a bow tie. *La Femme Élégante
à Paris*, 1926

1286   1287

Above
A design for a coat and a skirt suit.
La Femme Élégante à Paris, 1926

1282　　　　　　　　1283

Above and right
A design for a coat and a skirt suit.
La Femme Élégante à Paris, 1926

Two designs for skirt suits.
La Femme Élégante à Paris, 1926

1270   1271

1262   1263

1266   1267

1292   1293

Left
A checked walking suit and a green
walking suit with diamond shaped
button detailing. *La Femme Élégante
à Paris*, 1926

Above left and right
Two coats with pleats.
La Femme Élégante à Paris, 1926

Motoring coat and skirt suit.
La Femme Élégante à Paris, 1926

Outerwear

1274   1275

Left and below
Two walking suits. *La Femme Élégante
à Paris*, 1926

Various summer coat and skirt
suit designs. *La Femme Élégante
à Paris*, 1926

280

Below
Various summer coat and skirt
suit designs. *La Femme Élégante
à Paris*, 1926

Right
Pink spring coat in Kashalyne and
a blue Kashafyl dress with pink
scallops by Atelier Bachroitz.
Grande mode Parisienne, 1926

Grande Mode Parisienne

Atelier Bachwitz

ÉDITÉ EN AUTRICHE

London
28, South Molton Street.

Paris
64, Rue des Petits-Champs, 64.

Wien
111. Löwengasse 4?.

Right
Two wool crêpe walking suits.
La Femme Élégante à Paris, 1926

1268   1269

363

363 Ensemble élégant. Jaquette de velours foncé, remontant devant. Un pli crevé au milieu du dos. Fourrure claire. Robe en drap satin. Corsage drapé par un motif brodé au cordonnet. Boutons boules. Jupe rapportée avec pli crevé devant.

Atelier Bachroitz

Left and above
A model showing off over-the-knee
gaiters at the British Industry Fair,
c.1926

An ensemble of a red-brown satin with
a matching jacket of velvet trimmed with
light-coloured fur by Atelier Bachroitz
Modèles Originaux, c.1926

Outerwear

Right
Knitted day coat by Pierce Tex,
possibly a golfing coat. USA, c.1926

FAMOUS
PIERCE
TEX
FROM TO YOU
IN STEP WITH FASHION

Coat Style 10

Underwood & Underwood

Right
Two summer ensembles; the model
on the left is wearing a grey Georgette
and lace two-piece suit trimmed with
grey fox fur, the model on the right is
wearing a black and biscuit net dress
with three-tier frill effect and accordion
pleats. The collar is made of foxaline,
a cheaper pelt dyed to resemble fox
fur, c.1926

Above

Cover of *La Femme Chic à Paris*,
November 1926

Left and right
Italian advertisement for Lorenzo
Galtrucco fabrics featuring three
women in fashionable day dress,
c.1926

Travelling coat in herringbone tweed.
La Femme Chic, 1926

Fur-trimmed ensemble with crêpe
de Chine dress by Redfern. *La Femme
Chic*, 1926

Above
Three travelling ensembles by Berthe
Hermance. *La Femme Chic*, 1926

Outerwear

1998 Ensemble d'après-midi en velours. Veste vague garnie de renard. Haut de la robe en lamé et satin. Jupe formant pan du côté gauche.

1999 Ensemble en velours. Jaquette vague garnie de renard clair, tresse de soie et boutons passementerie. Robe avec trois volants en forme. Boucle métal.

Atelier Bachroitz

Left and above
A heavily embroidered spring coat worn
with a wide-brimmed hat, 1927

Velvet afternoon suit with a short coat
faced with fox fur, a dress with metal
lamé top and dark satin strips, a velvet
ensemble with an open jacket faced
with fox fur and a tiered dress by
Atelier Bachroitz. *Chic Parisien Beaux-
Arts des Modes*, 1927

Outerwear

2026 Manteau de visite en burafyl. Col drapé et garniture de nutria. Bandes rapportées au devant, aux manches et dans le dos.

2027 Manteau de promenade en velours. Col, parements et bordure de renard clair. Bas rapporté, froncé et remontant devant.

Atelier Bachroitz

Above and right

Afternoon coat edged with fur, and a velvet promenade coat edged with fox fur by Atelier Bachroitz. *Chic Parisien Beaux-Arts des Modes*, 1927

Actress Constance Talmadge wearing a satin-collared coat and cloche hat, 1927

The new SILHOUETTE from PARIS!

3HOI 3HO2 All-Wool LUSTRO SUEDE or BROADCLOTH $19.98 MAKES $55

6HOI 6HO2 All-Silk CANTON CREPE $7.98 MAKES $14

Descriptions on page two

HAMILTON GARMENT CO. FIFTH AVENUE NEW YORK

Left and above

Ira Richards at a horse show wearing a knitted jumper with abstract motif and a woollen skirt suit, accessorized with a mink stole and a large floral corsage, 1929

A fur-trimmed coat with scalloped panels and a day dress with a scarf capelet, cravat and a pointed skirt. *The New Silhouette from Paris*, Hamilton Garment Co. New York catalogue, c.1929

1920s Eveningwear

Below
'La Lettre Surprise' (The Surprise
Letter), illustration by Fernand Simeon.
Gazette du Bon Ton, 1920

Below
'Que vas-tu faire!' (What are you
going to do!), evening dress by Worth.
Illustration by Etienne Drian. *Gazette
du Bon Ton*, 1920

QUE VAS-TU FAIRE!

Robe du soir, de Worth

Right

Four evening dresses 'to see in the New Year' by Agnès, Rolf and Berthe Hermance, c.1920. *Le Femme Chic*, c.1920. The evening coat trimmed in fur and accessorized with a fur muff is by Agnès. The dresses have clear Oriental and exotic influences, with the pink and yellow models having harem and slave girl references in their design, embellishment and accessories. The fringes and sashes are very Mata Hari-esque, revealing that the famed performer and exotic dancer remained a figure of fascination even after her execution in 1917 for alleged spying.

Above
An evening dress of black and grey
patterned silk with a sash of black silk
by Redfern. *Paris Élégant*, 1920

Above
A luxurious evening dress with draped
ruches and 'Elizabeth' collar by Martial
et Armand. *Paris Élégant*, 1920

Right
An evening dress by Worth.
Gazette du Bon Ton, 1920

UNE ROBE DU SOIR DE WORTH

9787

le drapé nouveau. Création Callots.

GASTON DROUET, Éditeur.

6. Rue Ventadour. PARIS

Reproduction interdite

Paris Élégant

Supplément au N° 130- 1920

PL 1099

15

Above

A black evening dress with a fitted
bodice and draped skirt by the Soeurs
Callot. *Paris Élégant*, 1920

Below
'La Soubrette Annamite' (The Ladies'
Maid from Indochina), evening dress
with sash by Doeuillet. Illustration By
André Edouard Marty. *Gazette du Bon
Ton*, 1920

LA SOUBRETTE ANNAMITE

Robe du soir de Dœuillet, garnie de ruban

Right
A black pleated dress with voile
sleeves by Dorat, a blue petalled
evening gown with a voile train, a
mustard yellow dress with black
embellished voile panels and sleeves,
a black fan dress by Premet and a
dark blue woollen coat and skirt by
Beer. *La Femme Chic*, c.1920

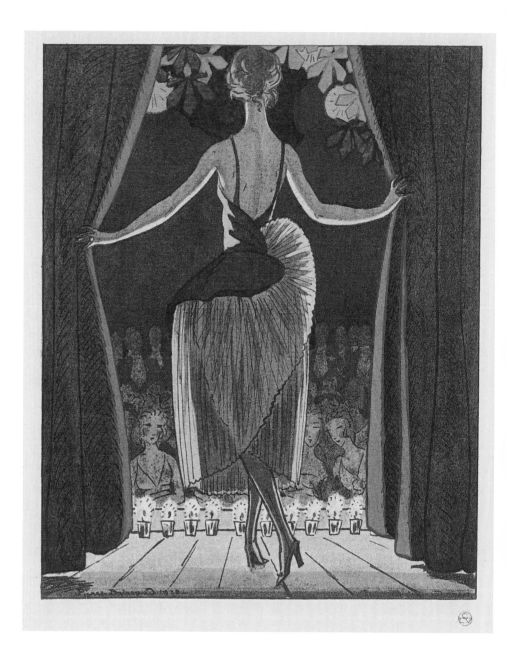

'Le Prologue ou La Comedie au
Chateau' (The Grand Opening),
design for a stage dress. Illustration
by Pierre Brissaud. *Gazette du
Bon Ton*, 1920

A collection of silk blouses. The
designs on various of the blouses
shows the exotic influences so
popular in the previous decade.
Paris-Blouses, 1920.

Eveningwear

3178

3179

3181

3180

3182

Le Charme des Tissus soyeux.

ÉTÉ 1920

PL 4

3510

3511

3509

3512

PL 6

Reproduction interdite

HIVER · 1920 · 1921

Supplément au N° 11

Les jolis Tea Gowns

Paris - Blouses.

Gaston DROUET, Éditeur.

6, Rue Ventadour, PARIS (1er arr)

Les Blouses de Dentelles.

Paris-Blouses.

Reproduction interdite

Gaston DROUET, Editeur

Supplément au N° 10

6, Rue Ventadour. PARIS (1ᵉʳ ᴀʀᴛ)

ÉTÉ 1920

Far left and left

Four French 'pretty' tea gowns in pink, yellow and purple, some with lace panelling and artificial flower detailing. Tea gowns were a late 19th century English invention, but the vogue for comfortable un-corseted afternoon dresses, initially only worn in the intimacy of one's own home, was quickly taken up by the French. By the 1920s the tea gown had moved out of the boudoir and the drawing room into more public spheres. *Paris-Blouses*, 1920-21

A collection of lace blouses. *Paris-Blouses*, 1920.

Croquis Pl_18   WORTH   WOR

321

Left
Two silhouettes by Worth and one by Beer. These drawings were presented as *Croquis*, quick sketchy drawings of live models and are very different and more fluid than the *Bon Ton*'s more formal fashion plates. *Gazette du Bon Ton*, 1920

BEER

GA
Bo

Eveningwear

Groquis
Pl-20

Jeanne Lanvin

Beer

GAZETTE DU
Bon Ton Nº 3

Above
Two silhouettes by Jeanne Lanvin and
one by Beer. The Oriental influences
of the Lanvin silhouettes are mirrored
in the models' depiction and styling.
Gazette du Bon Ton, c.1920

PAUL POIRET

LANVIN

Pl .17

Gazette du BonTon   N° 3   1920

Above
Two evening dresses by Paul Poiret
and a day ensemble by Jeanne
Lanvin. The Poiret dresses present
a contemporary use of historic
influences: the dress on the left is a
stylised modern version of a Greek
chiton, and the dress on the right
takes inspiration both for the silhouette
and the decorated skirt panel from 18th
century pannier dresses. The Lanvin
model draws inspiration from the 19th
century sailor suit. *Gazette du Bon
Ton*, 1920

Right
Evening ensemble by Worth.
L'Illustration des Modes, 1920

Next page
'Une Fête de Venise' (Venice Festival)
– black evening dress with green
scarf by Worth, pink silk dress by
Poiret, silver and diamanté dress by
Beer, yellow dress with green motifs
by Martial et Armand, and evening
ensemble with satin and fur coat by
Doeuillet. *L'Illustration des Modes*,
1920

Première Année. — N° 2.   REVUE BI-MENSUELLE   Jeudi 4 Novembre 1920

L'ILLUSTRATION
DES MODES
Lucien Vogel Directeur

" MON MANTEAU..." ou LE DÉPART DES INVITÉS
Un Ensemble pour le Soir, de Worth (11)

Prix du Numéro : 2 fr. 50.   13, Rue St-Georges, Paris.

Pl 19   Doeuillet

WORTH

GAZETTE DU
Bon Ton N° 3

Two evening gowns by Doeuillet and one by Worth. The models' nonchalant poses are typical of the way women were represented in graphic design, including fashion illustration in the first half of the 1920s. *Gazette du Bon Ton*, 1920

Right
A woman in a white evening dress
embellished with black beaded
fringes. *La Mode*, 1921

La Mode

Rédactrice en Chef : COUSINE JEANNE.

Nº 52 — 25 Décembre 1921 32 Pages. -- 50 Cantimes

Numéro de Noël : 8 pages de plus, 50 centimes. -- Attention ! ne pas couper la planche de travaux

Right
Five designs for the first cold days –
a voluminous grey coat by Morand, a
'cache coeur' evening dress, a black
panelled dress by Martial et Armand,
a black dress with an ornate Russian-
style jacket, and a fur-trimmed brown
coat by Morand. *La Femme Chic*,
c.1921

334

2202
2203
2204

Pl. 213

Nos élégantes au Cirque Molier

Paris Élégant

GASTON DROUET, Éditeur
6, Rue Ventadour, PARIS

Reproduction interdite

Supplément au N° 143 - 1921

Above
Three evening dresses modeled at
the private Cirque Molier, a highlight
in the Parisian social calendar. *Paris
Élégant*, 1921

2205

2206

2207

2208

Melle *Garat.*

Melle *Nina Myral.*

Melle *Garat.*

Melle *Miron*

Pℛ. 220

Première au Casino de Paris
Modèles Alice Bernard

Reproduction interdite

GASTON DROUET, Editeur

6 Rue Ventadour, PARIS

Paris Élégant

Supplément au N° 143-1921

Above
Four evening dresses by Alice
Bernard represented on contemporary
actresses and models who premiered
the gowns at the Casino de Paris.
Paris Élégant, 1921

Eveningwear

Above
Photograph of a model posing at
a fashion fair in a Richard Hickson
gown of jade green silk accessorized
with silk sash, artificial flowers and
a cuff around her arm. The model is
said to have received more marriage
proposals than any other
girl in America. c.1921

Above

'Venez Danser' (Come Dancing),
evening dress by Jeanne Lanvin,
illustration by Pierre Brissaud. Both
the design and the name of the
dress refer to the 1920s craze for
new dances such as the Charleston,
Foxtrot and Black Bottom which were
far more energetic than dances from
previous generations and so required
looser flowing gowns. *Gazette du Bon
Ton*, 1921

Above

'La Belle Dame sans Merci' (The Beautiful Lady without Mercy), evening dress by Worth. Illustration by George Barbier. The mythical Belle Dame sans Merci derives her name from a 15th century poem. She went on to inspire poets such as John Keats as well as Pre-Raphaelite artists and by 1921 was an established term for a femme fatale. *Gazette du Bon Ton*, 1921

Right and next page

A silk damask grey and light green evening dress with a gathered tablier. *Dernières Créations*, c.1923

Five dresses for holidays on the Côte d'Azur. Several of the dresses show classic Greek influences which are enforced by the models' poses and the backdrop of a classical colonnade. *La Femme Chic*, c.1922

S. 19

Below
'En plein cœur' (Shot through the
Heart), evening dress by Paul Poiret.
Illustration by André Edouard Marty.
Gazette du Bon Ton, 1922

EN PLEIN CŒUR

ROBE DU SOIR, DE PAUL POIRET

Above
A lavender blue crêpe de Chine ball
dress with a pleated flounced skirt.
Dernières Créations, c.1923

Right
Hollywood actress Pauline Frederick
wearing a brocade satin evening gown
with crystal trimmings, accesorised
with a large marabou fan, a gold leaf
head band and satin shoes, c.1922

Above
A blue crêpe de Chine evening dress finished with grey velvet flowers and a worsted girdle of grey and silver ribbon. *Dernières Créations*, c.1923

Right
Woman wearing a blue evening dress with bell sleeves and a large white fur trim. *Nouvelle Mode*, 1923

348

Above left and right
A black moiré evening dress with a
large blue floral corsage at the waist
and matching ruffed cuffs. *Dernières
Créations*, c.1923

A gold and black lamé evening dress
with a pointed skirt draped on the hips.
Dernières Créations, c.1923

Eveningwear

S. 24

Right
A black and gold broched silk theatre
wrap with an ape skin collar. *Dernières
Créations*, c.1923

A lilac silk evening dress draped at the
front and held by a darker bow worn
over a silver lace underslip. *Dernières
Créations*, c.1923

Below
A silver lace evening dress with
a large embroidered front panel with
pearls and a silk tassel. *Dernières
Créations*, c.1923

S. 17

Right
A red silk cashmere party dress with
a large skirt sash tied at the back as
a large loop. *Dernières Créations*,
c.1923

S. 1

Below left and right
A maize yellow Marocain crêpe
evening dress with wide velvet orange
waist ribbons. *Dernières Créations*,
c.1923

A silk cashmere evening dress with
a pleated skirt held on the hips.
Dernières Créations, c.1923

Right
A crêpe Georgette evening dress with a
fox fur skirt border. *Dernières Créations*,
c.1923

S. 20

Below left and right
A light silk ball dress with lace flounce
and bow and two sloping flounces on
the skirt. *Dernières Créations*, c.1923

A rose 'picture' dress with an
appliqued lace skirt. *Dernières
Créations*, c.1923

Below left and right
A crêpe de Chine dancing dress with side lace panels. *Dernières Créations*, c.1923

A rose silk and crêpe Georgette dancing dress with a flounced collar and skirt. *Dernières Créations*, c.1923

Below
A green moiré dress with fur-trimmed
skirt flounces and a shoulder
shawl tied at the back. *Dernières
Créations*, c.1923

Below
A turquoise silk ball dress with
a black silk overskirt. *Dernières
Créations*, c.1923

Below
A Parisian evening dress of blue and white crêpe de Chine with a figured pattern worked on the waistline and the skirt. A narrow scarf of blue crêpe with an artificial large rose is worn around the neck, c.1923

Right
Pink picture-style evening gown with large bow and lacing at the back, c.1923

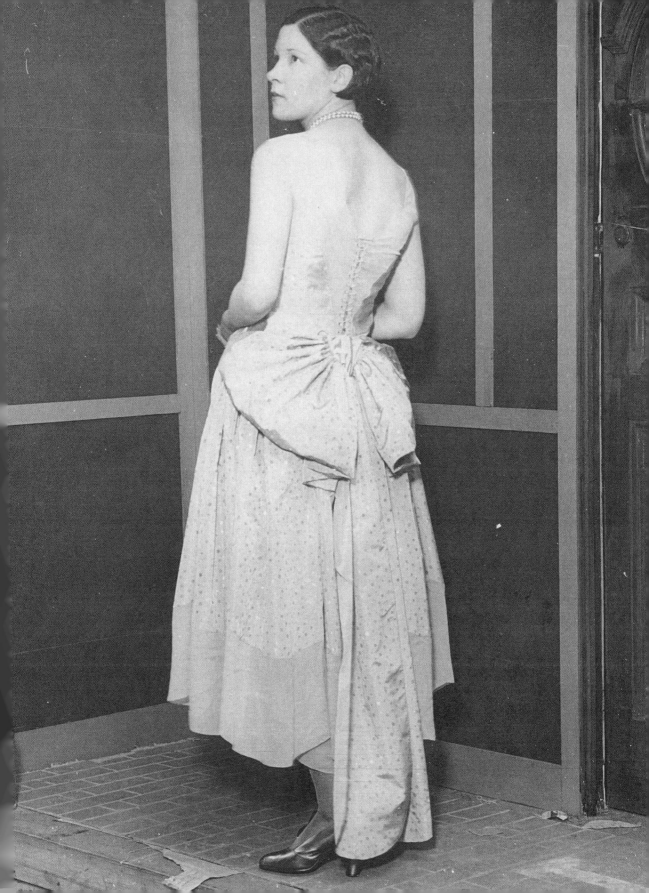

Above
A woman wearing a fur-trimmed
tunic worn over a skirt and belted
with a band of fabric embellished
with artificial leaves, c.1923

Above
A silver lamé and green moiré evening
dress with skirt flounces. *Dernières
Créations*, c.1923

Right
Extravagant stage costume, lavishly
embellished with pearl and bead
embroideries and complimented with
a wraparound opera coat equally richly
decorated. The headdress is made of
pheasant feathers and long multiple
strands of pearls, while a variety of
diamanté bracelets complete the look.
Paramount Pictures, c.1924

Right
French film actress Arlette Marchal
dressed in a chiffon negligée dress
worn with a metallic lace coat and an
ostrich feather boa accesorised with
a tight-fitting turban hat and satin silk
shoes with diamantée clasps, c.1924

62473

Above and right

Actress Helena D'Algy in one of her costumes from *Confessions of a Queen*, 1925

'Golconde' gold lamé cape coat with skunk-trimmed sleeves and scarf, c.1925. The name of the dress probably refers to the Indian city of Golconda which was once famed for its diamond mines. By the late 19th Century, the word Golconda had come to signify 'something associated with great wealth', and so the name fits perfectly with the idea of a gold outfit.

Above and Left
A model wearing a black Panne velvet
dress and cape trimmed with black fox
fur, c.1925

A tiered printed taffeta evening
gown with a beaded and fringed
scarf, c.1925

Right
A gold brocade evening coat with
a large multicoloured collar and a
pink and grey dancing dress. *Paris
Élégant*, c.1925

9263

9264

Très élégant ensemble pour le soir créé par Mariette Pognot.

GASTON DROUET, Éditeur - Gérant
29, rue de la Sourdière,
PARIS (1er)

PARIS-ÉLÉGANT
Supplément au N° 230. — Pl. 565
Reproduction interdite

Left
Actress Helena D'Algy in one of her costumes from *Confessions of a Queen*, 1925

Below
A ball gown of gold lace worn over a gold lamé slip dress with a matching fringed scarf, and a ball dress of crêpe de Chine with richly beaded embroidery by Atelier Bachroitz. *Chic Parisien Beaux-arts des modes*, 1925

No 328
11

„Chic Parisien"

873

874

Atelier Bachroitz

Modèles Originaux

342

342 Robe du soir en lamé côtelé et velours chiffon deux couleurs.
Tunique brodée corail et jais.

Atelier Bachroitz

Above
Evening dress of ribbed silver
lamé and chiffon velvet in blue
and black by Atelier Bachroitz
Modèles Originaux, c.1926

Modèles Originaux

Modèles Originaux

Above left and right

Black dancing dress in chiffon velvet with crossed back and sash by Atelier Bachroitz. *Modèles Originaux*, c.1926. The belt and detailing are of paste embroidery and the model is wearing slave bracelets on one arm, a fashion in keeping with exotic influences, which moved from all-over dress designs to detailing by the middle of the decade.

Black chiffon velvet and gold lamé evening dress with a design for breeches in the background by Atelier Bachroitz. *Modèles Originaux*, c.1926. The dress is draped in a knot-like manner at the front to create the pointed silhouette, while the central part of the knot is embroidered with pearls.

Right and next page
Five dresses by Georgette and a navy
dress with mustard trim by Dupony. *La
Femme Chic*, 1926

Seven evening dresses by Atelier
Bachroitz. *Chic Parisien Beaux-Arts
des Modes*, c.1926.The dresses show
the wide variety of fashionable styles
on offer, from tiered romantic lace
dresses, to fur-trimmed sash dresses,
richly embellished sack dresses and
black evening dresses in lace or with
low-cut backs.

864

865

866

867

868

869

870

Atelier Bachroitz

Beaux-Arts des Modes

50ᶜ NOUVELLE MODE 50

Pour les nouvelles conditions
d'abonnement à l'étranger,
voir page 5

Publications V. DE NOIRFONTAINE, 5. Boulevard des Capucines Paris.

Above and right
Woman in an evening dress with a
run-through neck scarf and pleated
skirt. *Nouvelle Mode*, 1926

A woman in a low-waisted green
dress with a deep v-neckline.
Nouvelle Mode, 1926

Previous page
'Dresses in all styles', black evening
gown with loops of pearls and
sequinned pink evening gown by
Eugénie et Juliette; fur-trimmed
ensemble, black day dress and
maroon ensemble by Alice Bernard;
yellow evening gown with artificial
roses and black velvet and pink satin
evening gown by Alice Bernard.
La Femme Chic, 1926

Eveningwear

Pour les nouvelles conditions
d'abonnement à l'étranger,
voir page 5

251

Publications V. DE NOIRFONTAINE, 5. Boulevard des Capucines Paris.

„Chic Parisien"

Above

Three evening dresses by Atelier
Bachroitz. *Chic Parisien Beaux-Arts
des Modes*, c.1927. The marabou
feather fan was a popular accessory
and its gold detailing matches the
floral embellishment of the dress.
The middle dress has a long train
affixed with a large bow. This style
of dress became popular in the
second half of the decade.

875

876

Atelier Bachroitz

Above

Two Atelier Bachroitz evening dresses.
Chic Parisien Beaux-Arts des Modes,
c.1927. The model on the left is a
wrap-over design which affixes at the
waist and the right model has a deep
cut v-shaped back and is embellished
with snowflake designs, a large
embellished bow and trimmed in fur.

Eveningwear

2014 Robe à danser en velours souple. Corsage très croisé. Plastron de dentelle
métal. Roses de lamé. Pan doublé de même. Trois volants en forme.

2015 Princesse en fulgurante claire. A droite un lé de satin foncé, se terminant
en trois pans arrondis brodés bijoux et perles. Du côté gauche un drapé
doublé de satin noir.

2010 Robe demi-style en taffetas. Devant droit replié en revers. Plastron de dentelle métal. Jupe coulissée.

2011 Robe du soir en Georgette. Jupe très mouvementée. Bande cernant le décolleté et motifs brodés métal et perles.

Atelier Bachroitz

Opposite left and above

Velour dancing dress with a crossed bodice and metal vestee, and a princess evening robe of fulgurante with dark satin scallops trimmed with beading and rhinestone embroidery by Atelier Bachroitz. *Chic Parisien Beaux-Arts des Modes*, 1927

Demi-style taffeta dress with metal lace, and a Georgette evening dress embroidered with metal and pearls by Atelier Bachroitz. *Chic Parisien Beaux-Arts des Modes*, 1927

2028 Robe du soir en satin. Volant simulant boléro, rapporté en biais. Ceinture
écharpe de tissu. Jupe ondulante, allongée et formant godets du côté gauche.

2029 Robe à danser en crêpe de Chine clair. Bandes de tissu disposées en largeur.
Ceinture avec boucle bijouterie. Jupe mouvementée. Lé drapé formant pans.

Atelier Bachroitz

Above

Black satin evening dress, and a
pale crêpe de Chine dancing frock
by Atelier Bachroitz. *Chic Parisien
Beaux-Arts des Modes*, 1927

2012 Robe à danser en crêpe Georgette sur fond de satin. Haut jaboté à droite. Ceinture écharpe de faille. Tablier tunique ondulant appliqué en biais, long pan du côté gauche.

2013 Robe du soir en dentelle soie délicate. Corsage croisé. Nœud de satin avec long pan, fixé par une grosse rose. Jupe étroite de satin. Deux volants de dentelle, brodés métal.

Atelier Bachroitz,

Above
Georgette dancing frock worn over a satin slip, and a silk lace evening dress with a crossed bodice and a tight fitting skirt covered with lace flounces by Atelier Bachroitz. *Chic Parisien Beaux-Arts des Modes*, 1927

Eveningwear

Right
Hollywood actress Agnes Ayres in a
white chiffon dress trimmed with black
and white paillettes by Lambert. The
dress was a costume she wore in the
1927 comedy *Eve's Love Letters*.
1927

2032

2032

2033

2033

Atelier Bachroitz

2032 Robe de style en tulle soie ou mousseline sur fond de taffetas. Corsage
très échancré dans le dos, retenu par quatre bretelles. Ample jupe plus
longue dans le dos que devant et garnie de ruches de tissu. Deux roses de
soie à la hanche gauche.

2033 Robe de style en taffetas fleur. Corsage en pointe avec petit décolleté. Jupe
étagée, bords de tulle. Plaques bijouterie

2024 Robe du soir en Georgette. Mi-boléro rapporté en biais. Lé formant
pointe et drapé, remontant à gauche. Broderie or. Une rose à la ceinture.

2025 Robe à danser en crêpe de Chine formée de bandes rapportées, drapées
à la partie inférieure et arrondies à l'ourlet.

Left and above
Pink frock in silk net bolstered by
a foundation of taffetas, and a black
taffeta frock bordered with net
by Atelier Bachroitz. *Chic Parisien
Beaux-Arts des Modes*, 1927

Georgette dancing dress with gold
embroidery, and a dancing frock
with bands of crêpe de Chine joined
together by Atelier Bachroitz. *Chic
Parisien Beaux-Arts des Modes*, 1927

396

Right
Georgette evening dress with a
pleated skirt and curved edges, a
chiffon velour and lace evening gown,
a crêpe princess dress with bead
embroidered bolero, a crêpe dancing
frock with draped side wings, a
taffeta evening dress with draped side
wings, a taffeta evening dress with
lace vestee and strass embroidery, a
demi-style dress in black net, and a
Georgette dancing frock with a bolero
of metal lace by Atelier Bachroitz. *Chic
Parisien Beaux-Arts des Modes*, 1927

2034

2035

2034

2035

2036

2037

2036

2036 Rol
        Bo

2037 Rol

2038 Rol
        pa

.2034 Robe du soir en Georgette brodée de tubes et perles d'or. Haut de genre
        boléro. Jupe plissée à bord festonnant. Touffe de roses de soie.

.2035 Toilette de soirée en velours chiffon. Corsage croisé. Bas de genre casaque,
        se terminant en pan du côté gauche. Plastron et bas de jupe en dentelle
        de soie sur fond de lamé. Echarpe de dentelle.

2037

2038

2039

2040

2038

2039

2040

Atelier Bachwitz

in. Côté drapé formant pan. Boléro perlé.

ol. Ailes de côté drapées. Boucle bijouterie.

u côté droit un lé ondulant se terminant en
rodé de pierres pareilles

2039 Robe demi=style en tulle noir. Jupe volantée remontant à gauche. Corsage
garni d'applications de tulle. Ceinture de ruban avec rose de couleur.

2040 Robe à danser en Georgette. Boléro de dentelle métal. Bandes incrustées
à la taille et bordures des volants de jupe également de dentelle métal.

Above
Five dresses by Parisian couturiers
Jane Regny, Jenny, Bernard et
Cie, Redfern and Suzanne Talbot.
Sélection, c.1927

Eveningwear

Right
Beaded evening dress and black
velvet dress. *Fashion for All*, 1927

402

Above
American designer Marion Stehlik
wearing one of her own creations
made of lace with an Elizabethan-style
collar, c.1927

Below
Georgette evening dress embroidered
with multicoloured tinsels, and
an informal satin evening robe
embroidered with a flower border
on the left and back by Atelier
Bachroitz. *Chic Parisien Beaux-Arts
des Modes*, 1927

2002 Robe du soir en crêpe Georgette. Libellule brodée de paillettes de couleurs.
Jupe formant pans du côté droit.

2003 Robe de petit soir en satin. Bordure de fleurs brodée perles. Décolleté rond
devant, en V dans le dos. Dos croisé. Pans flottants des deux côtés.

2022 Robe à danser en taille taffetas et tulle. Tablier original. Bordure et em-
piécement de hanches brodés de perles et tubes. Cordelière pareille cernant
l'échancrure en pointe, long gland. Ceinture de tissu avec boucle de perles.

2023 Robe à danser en crêpe mongol. Echancrure ovale. Plastron en lamé argent.
Volants en forme et écharpe doublés de même. Boucle bijouterie.

Atelier Bachroitz

Above
Faille and tulle dancing frock
with tasseled and embroidered
detailing, and a crêpe dancing
dress with bell shaped flounces
by Atelier Bachroitz. *Chic Parisien
Beaux-Arts des Modes*, 1927

Right
Satin evening dress with a bolero
shaped top, a circular yoke and a
lace lower part, and a dancing frock
in metal lace on a satin slip by Atelier
Bachroitz. *Chic Parisien Beaux-Arts
des Modes*, 1927

Eveningwear

2006

2007

2006 Robe du soir en satin. Haut de genre boléro se continuant à gauche en un lé drapé. Empiècement rond et bas de jupe en dentelle de soie. Bouquet d'épaule.

2007 Robe à danser en dentelle métal sur fond de satin. Ceinture pareille avec boucle bijouterie. Jupe à trois volants se terminant en pointes du côté droit. Echarpe de dentelle, fixée à l'épaule gauche par un chrysanthème.

Atelier Bachwitz

1920s Accessories

Le Nº : 50 Cent.

24ᵉ Année. – Nº 49 – 28 Novembre 1920

★ ★ ★ – 24 pages

La Mode

Parure
nouvelle
en fourrure
✧✧✧

Dans
ce numéro,
son explication
✧✧✧

Rédactrice en chef :
COUSINE JEANNE

Prix des abonnements

FRANCE ET COLONIES		UNION POSTALE	
7 francs	3 mois	8 francs	
13 francs	6 mois	14 francs	
25 francs	Un an	27 francs	

Hôtel du PETIT JOURNAL
61, rue Lafayette
PARIS

Left and right
Woman wearing a black opera coat
with a fur collar, accessorized with
a matching fur turban-style hat and
muff. *La Mode*, 1920

Silent film actress Mary Anderson in
a blue and grey woven day dress and
a blue and white hat with a large pearl
hatpin, c.1921

Above and right
'Latest Fashions' in hats. The
pyramid-like hats were derived from
traditional festive Russian kokoshnik
headdresses and reflect the impact
of Russian émigré designers on
Parisian fashions. *La Nouveauté
Francaise*, 1921.

Postcard of a woman in a blue
ensemble with an exotic scarf, 1922

412

Below and right

Four summer dresses in crêpe,
embroidered in a variety of designs
and colours. *The Ladies' Home Journal*,
1922 – with a prerequisite parasol

Crocheted and knitted fashions
and accessories, *Woman's Home
Companion*, 1922

Spring Smartness Phrased in Wool

Cleverly knit and crocheted for sports and street wear

Designed by HELEN MARVIN

B

THE significant thing about this coat sweater is the panel-scarf - collar, which flings itself warmly back against a girl's throat and over one shoulder.

TO SHADE the eyes when motoring or hiking, this little sports hat of flame-colored floss is effective. The corded effect is obtained by working single crochet over a chain-stitch cord of knitting worsted. A band of wooden beads adds a voguish note.

A

The panel scarf of the coat sweater as it hangs straight

Below, back of the vestee at the left, with strap buttoning it to the front

C

D

Crocheted flowers and leaves, and a loop-stitch fringe trim this colorful scarf and hat of soft Jack-rose duvetyn

VERY chic is this tailored little reindeer-gray vest, banded with a delicate shade of silk and wool floss, to wear with a spring suit. Notice the cunning change pockets, and the small buttons in gold silk crochet.

THE directions for each of these garments may be obtained in convenient illustrated leaflet form, price 10 cents. The order number is CK-178. Please order by name as well as by number, A—scarf sweater, B—sports hat, C—vestee, D—scarf and hat trimmed with crocheted flowers and fringe. Address Knitting Department, Woman's Home Companion, 381 Fourth Avenue, New York City.

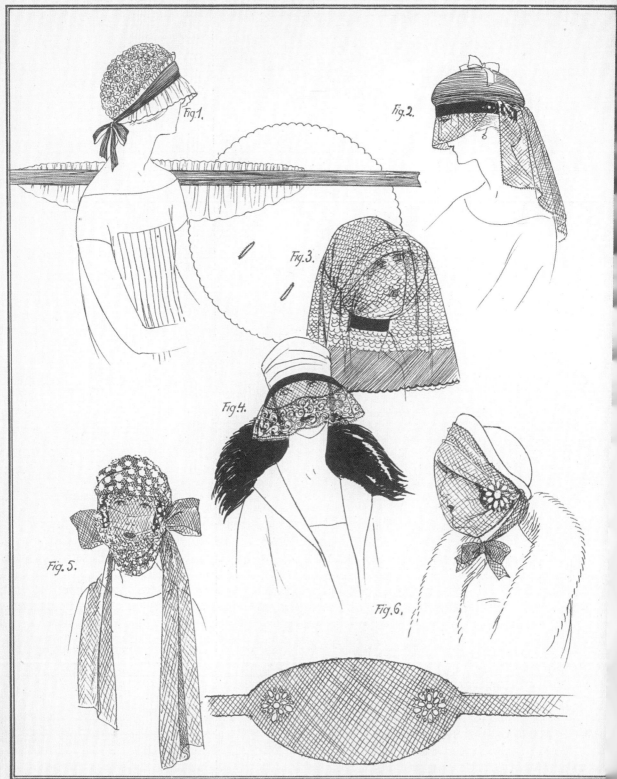

Fig.1.

Fig.2.

Fig.3.

Fig.4.

Fig.5.

Fig.6.

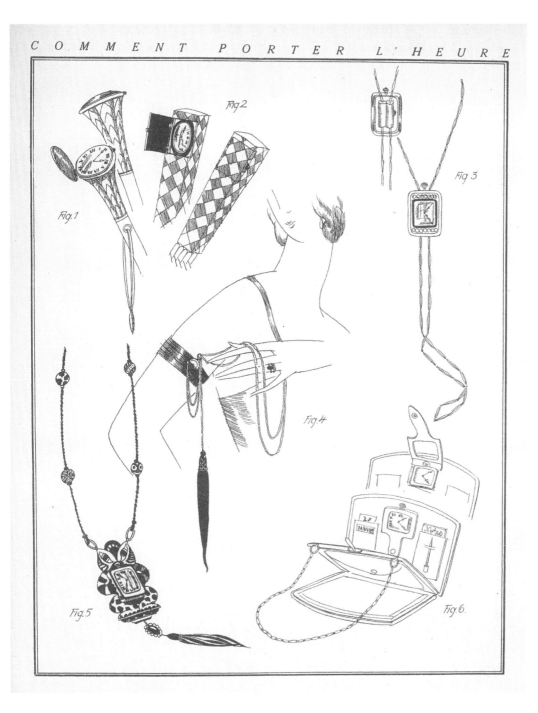

Left and above
Selection of fashionable veils.
Gazette du Bon Ton, 1922

Illustration of upmarket novelty
watches. *Gazette du Bon Ton*, 1922

Dres

Dress 3836

Blouse 3839
Hat 3665

Embroidery
design 10954

Dress 3841
Embroidery
design 10968

Other views are on page 87

Dress 3875

Dress 3842

Dress 3852

Dress 3845

Above

Designs for summer dresses
accompanied by a variety of
accessories. *The Delineator*, 1922

Accessories

Dress 3856

Dress 3843
Embroidery
design 10871

Dress 3873
Embroidery
design 10937

Dress 3879

Dress 3869

Blouse 3729

Other views are on page 88

Dress 3871
Embroidery
design 10895

Above
Designs for summer dresses
accompanied by a variety of
accessories. *The Delineator*, 1922

Accessories

1465

Paris-Chapeaux
29, RUE DE LA SOURDIÈRE
PARIS (1ᵉʳ arrᵗ)

Un original travail de paille d'Hélène Julien.

SUPPLÉMENT
Nᵒ 142 - PL 801

Left and above
Three creations by Parisian milliner
Jane Blanchot. *Les Chapeaux de
La Femme Chic*, c.1923

An original hat model constructed out
of burgundy straw by Parisian milliner
Hélène Julien, *Paris-Chapeaux*,
c.1923. Note the model's rouged
cheeks and red lipstick.

Below and left
Design for a wide brimmed hat.
Les Chapeaux du 'Trés Parisien',
1923-1924

A black satin afternoon coat studded
with white beads and trimmed with
a black fox collar and cuffs and worn
with a tight-fitting hat with plumes.
Central News photograph, c.1923

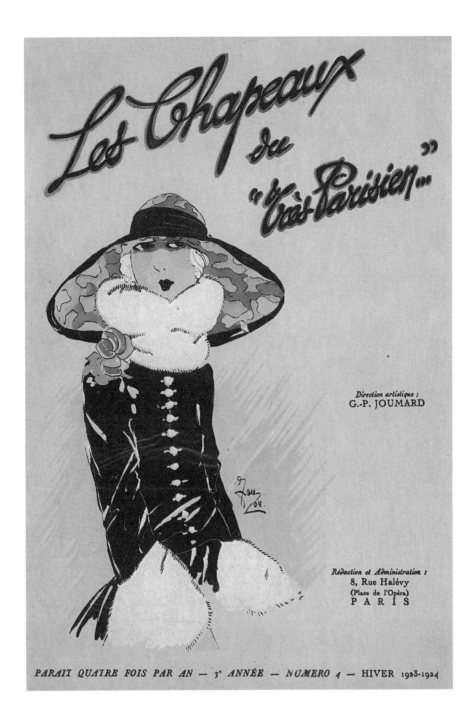

Right
Woman in a blue sweater dress
with matching scarf and toque
in multicoloured design. *Nouvelle
Mode*, 1924

Publications V. DE NOIRFONTAINE, 5. Boulevard des Capucines Paris.

1628

1629

1630

Aléxis

Paris-Chapeaux

Les chapeaux de deuil et leurs sobres garnitures

29, RUE DE LA SOURDIÈRE
PARIS (1ᵉʳ arrᵗ)

SUPPLÉMENT
Nᵒ 132 — PL. 654

Left and above

Three Parisian mourning hats, *Paris-Chapeaux* c.1924. The designs of the hats are very fashionable and it is only the long black veils that single them out as mourning attire.

Three creations by Parisian milliner Amicy Boinard. *Les Chapeaux de La Femme Chic*, c.1924

Below and right
A winter hat of dark straw trimmed
at the side with an ornament of ostrich
feathers. London, c.1924

A Parisian spring hat made of
'Bangkok Straw' and trimmed with
ruby-coloured velvet with a brim
lined to match the ribbon, c.1925

Below left and right
A spring hat made of picet-straw with a flat crown of rose-colored satin and finished off with a small diamanté buckle, c.1924

A navy blue hat made of corded ribbon in a close fitting cloche shape with a large beige velvet flower and an eye veil, c.1925. The vogue for of wearing multiple strands of pearls is accredited to Coco Chanel.

Below left and right
A large brimmed hat in pale green
crêpe de Chine with a bunch of
artificial flowers worn on the brim,
c.1925

A wide-brimmed hat of champagne-
coloured straw, piped with a ribbon
in a darker shade to match the satin
crown, which is elaborately trimmed
with embroidered gold brocade,
c.1924. The image is very similar to the
popular actresses postcards of the
time and shows that whilst the cloche
hat became the preferred choice
of headgear in the 1920s, more
romantic styles were equally popular.

Above
Selection of day hats.
Au Louvre catalogue, 1925

FORMES

77.461. FORME fillette en tagal noir, marron, gris, blond, marine, rouge, vieux rose, nattier, champagne ou blanc **8.75**
Entrées 53, 55, 57.
En paille fantaisie chinée marron/blond, marine/vert, rouge/noir, naturel/rouge ou écossais.

77.455. CHAPELIER paille exotique, noir, nègre, brûlé, rouge a marine **15.** »
13.25

La forme nue en paille anglaise, noir, nègre, brûlé, marine ou rouille.
9.75
En blanc **14.75**

77.471. PANAMA pour dame et grande fillette, belle qualité. **14.50**
Entrées 55 à 58.
Qualité plus fine. **21.** »

77.457. Grande CAPELINE en tagal picot, noir, marron, marine, blond, bué, gris, rouille et blanc, garniture ruban ottoman assorti. **26.** »
La forme nue en tagal picot **13.75**
La forme nue en liséré Japon, noir, marron ou naturel **10.75**

77.469. FORME paille exotique, imitation bangkok noir, nègre, mordoré ou rouge. **14.75**
En liséré, belle qualité, mêmes coloris. **12.90**

77.462. MARQUIS pour fillette en tagal picot, mêmes coloris unis que le 77.461 . . . **9.90**
Entrées 53, 55, 57.

77.463. Grande CAPELINE paille fantaisie ruban noir, marron, blond, marine, mauve, rouge ou blanc. **29.** »
Entrées 57 ou 59.
En tagal picot, mêmes coloris et mêmes entrées. **15.75**

77.470. FORME marquis en tagal picot noir, marron, mordoré, prune, marine a gris. **17.50**
En paille anglaise, belle qualité, mêmes coloris. **29.75**

77.468. FORME paille anglaise, très belle qualité, noir, marron, mordoré, marine, gris ou rouille. **28.75**
En tagal picot, mêmes coloris **16.90**

77.460. CHAPELIER imitation crin, en noir seulement. **19.50**
La forme nue, en tagal fantaisie crêpé, noir, nègre, mordoré, marine, gris, rouge, vert, blé ou blanc. **9.90**

77.467. FORME paille anglaise noir, nègre, rouge ou mordoré. **15.90**
En paille exotique Bowen, mêmes coloris. **11.75**

77.454. CHAPELIER souple, paille imitation manille, noir, nègre, rouge, mordoré, blanc. Entrée 57 ou 59 . . . . . **19.75**
En mi-feutre, très belle qualité, noir, marron, marine, gris, castor, rouge, beige ou blanc, ruban assorti, mêmes entrées. **21.** »

77.459. Grand CHAPELIER paille exotique brillante, noir, marron, blond, rouge ou blanc, garniture cocarde ruban assti. **29.** »
La forme nue, mêmes coloris **15.50**
La forme nue, en tagal picot, mêmes coloris . . **13.50**

77.453. DIRECTOIRE en paille exotique, pour dame ou fillette, bordure velours noir, motifs peinture à l'huile sur fond grège. **18.75**
Entrées 55, 57, 59.

77.465. FORME paille fantaisie dentelle noir, champagne, marron, castor ou blanc. **22.** »
En paille exotique genre bangkok, noir, marron ou mordoré. **12.75**

77.466. FORME paille exotique genre manille, marron, noir, rouge, blond, blé ou blanc. **14.90**
En tagal picot, mêmes coloris. **14.75**

77.473. Souple OTTOMAN noir, marine, marron, gris, castor, rouge, vieux rose, nattier, champagne ou blanc, broderie fantaisie **13.50**
Le même non brodé **8.50**
En peau brillante, non brodée, noir, cuir, nègre, rouge ou blanc **19.75**

77.474. SOUPLE en peau brillante noir, cuir, rouge, nègre ou blanc . . . **21.** »
En ottoman, mêmes coloris. **10.75**
En piqué blanc **6.90**

77.472. CAPELINE en blanc seulement, belle qualité . . **3.90**
CAPELINE paille Italie, nuance naturelle, sans franges, belle qualité **10.75**
Entrées 55, 57, 59.
Qualité plus fine **19.75**

Sauf indication contraire nos Formes et Chapeaux ne se font qu'en entrée de tête 59/60

Above
Selection of day hats.
Au Louvre catalogue, 1925

Left and above
Actress Mary Brian wearing a cloche
hat, a sports sweater and leather
fingerless golfing gloves, c.1925

Woman in a fashionable knitted tunic
suit, with matching hat and Bakelite
handbag. *Mode Pratique*, 1925

"GERDA" 20 bould Mor

N° 600 · ECHARPE

Très élégante, spéciale pour l'auto.

En très beau crêpe de chine, écossais, quatre nuances peintes à la main avec dessin de franges, sur fond : saumon, beige ou vert.

Dimensions :
1 m 70 × 0 m 48

Prix: frs **125.** »

600

601

RTRE **PARIS**

01 - CHALE

t. Cette mode règne
maître.

e brodé main qualité supé-
franges soie rapportées,
ail, nattier, champagne,

m × 1m plus franges 0m35.

Prix : frs **350.** "

N" 602 - ECHARPE

**Pour la ville, souple, utile
en toutes circonstances.**

Crêpe de chine belle qualité.
Fond blanc uni, bord impression
spéciale. Nuances : chinées.

Dimensions :
1m80 × 0m48 / 0m50

Prix : frs **99.** "

602

Left
Blouses and shawls by Maison Gerda.
Maison Gerda catalogue, c.1925

GERDA

Three evening dresses by Maison
Gerda. Maison Gerda Catalogue,
c.1925 – with fans including one made
from ostrich feathers

438

Below
Over-the-knee decorative jersey spatter dashers worn over leather heels. 'Spats' had traditionally been made of leather and were mostly worn by men to protect their shoes and trousers although they did have a decorative function. In the 1920s they became a purely decorative ladies fashion. USA, c.1925

Right
Anklets or decorative ankle bands worn over a nude shade of patterned stockings and with decorated leather strappy heels. USA, c.1925

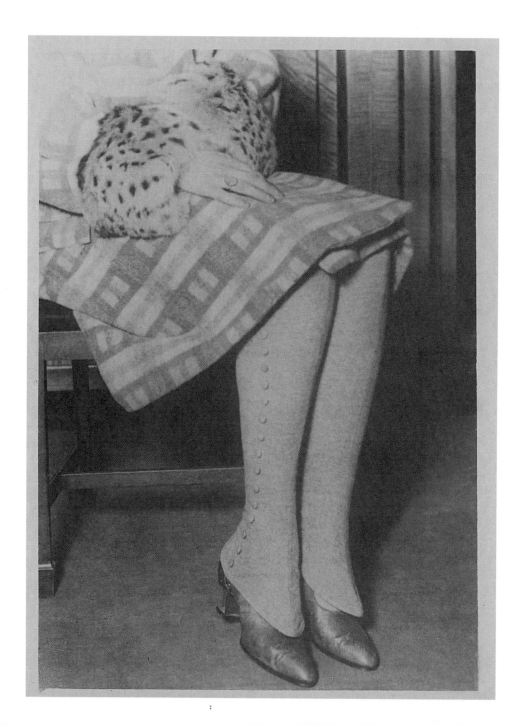

2701

Hélène Julien

Hélène Julien

2702

Rose Petit

2703

Quelques formes plus grandes.

Paris Chapeaux
29, rue de la Sourdière
PARIS

Sur. N° 177 Pl. 1026

Left and below
Three cloche hat designs by
Hélène Julien and Rose Petit.
Paris Chapeaux, c.1926

Woman wearing a black single-breasted
jacket over a white blouse and cloche
hat. *Nouvelle Mode*, 1926

Pour les nouvelles conditions
d'abonnement à l'étranger,
voir page 5

NOUVELLE MODE 50ᶜ

Nᵒ 9. — 28 Févr

Publications V. DE NOIRFONTAINE, 5. Boulevard des Capucines Paris.

Left and above
Actress Betty Bronson in the movie
Paradise wearing close-fitting hat
with ribbon banding, 1926

Woman at the races in floral crêpe
dress with pleated skirt, a dark blue
coat and an envelope bag. *Nouvelle
Mode*, 1926

Right
Cover of *La Femme Chic à Paris*,
July 1926

La femme chic

all. Jarach ? P. Chaumry.

Teléfono - 85-855
La femme chic

Right
Woman in a white summer dress
with a bold rose motif, pleated panels
and bell sleeves carrying a parasol.
Nouvelle Mode, 1926

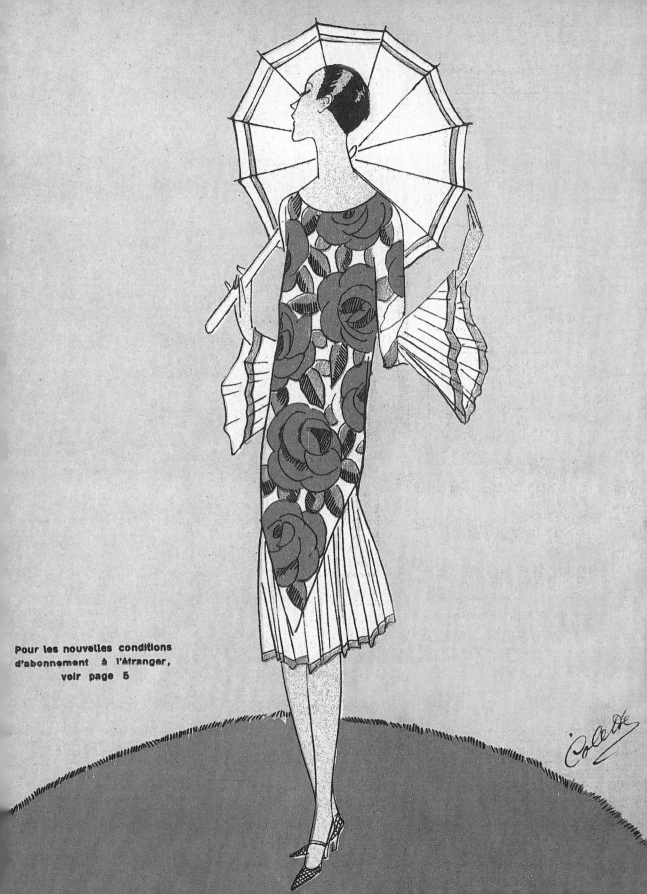

Pour les nouvelles conditions
d'abonnement à l'étranger,
voir page 5

Right
A luxurious evening gown in
diaphanous material cut into an
upwards v-shape at the front and
trimmed with panels of metallic
fabric. The top half of the dress
is made from the same material.
The style is finished off with a
floral fabric corsage and an ostrich
feather fan. London, c.1926

Les chapeaux
de 'La femme chic' Création Héléne Thibault Pl. 1
Supplément au N° 140
Imp. Lafontaine. Paris

Above
Black straw and fur hat by
Héléne Thibault, *Les Chapeaux
de 'La Femme Chic'*, 1927

Les chapeaux
de La femme chic
Supplément au N° 140

Créations Hélène Thibault

Pl. 5

Imp. Lafontaine. Paris

Above
Two cloche hats by Héléne
Thibault, *Les Chapeaux de
'La Femme Chic'*, 1927

Right
A creation by Reville of Hanover
Square, London – a close-fitting
almond green jumper matched
with motoring gauntlets, c.1928

Below
Selection of fashionable hats including
cloches, berets and tight-fitting skull
caps. *The New Silhouette from Paris*,
Hamilton Garment Co. New York
catalogue, c.1929

Selection of fashionable cloche hats.
The New Silhouette from Paris,
Hamilton Garment Co. New York
catalogue, c.1929

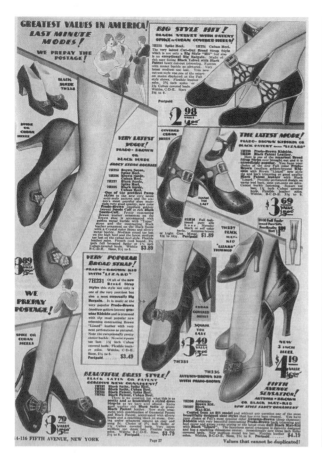

All Above
Selection of fashionable shoes.
The New Silhouette from Paris,
Hamilton Garment Co. New York
catalogue, c.1929

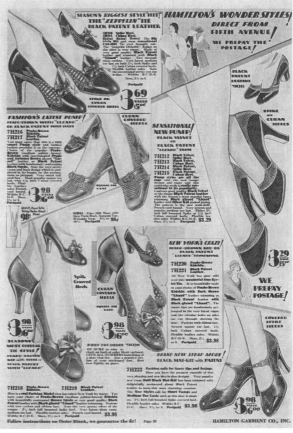

1920s Other

Below and right
Four French negligée designs with
luxurious lace, ribbon and flower
detailing. The Twenties saw a shift to
all-in-one undergarments. The model
on the right is wearing a lace bed
cap. *Paris-Blouses*, 1920

Four chemises with embroidery or
openwork detailing. *Paris-Blouses*,
1920

3547

3548

Right
Advertisement for the supple
and discreet 'Le Select' corset.
L'Illustration des Modes, 1920

"LE SELECT"
corset parisien par excellence

"Le Select" n'est plus le rigide corset
c'est un gracieux soutien souple et discret

en vente à paris dans les grands magasins du louvre et du printemps
et en province dans toutes les bonnes maisons

464

LIBRON & Cᵢₑ, Manufacture de Corsets, 54, Avenue de Clichy, PARIS

Other

Left
Corset advert 'for fashions to come, wear the supple Le Select corset'. This elasticated corselet flattened curves in order to provide the fashionable silhouette of the era. It was worn over a thin negligée and had suspender clips attached for stockings which had become increasingly popular owing to rising hemlines. *La Nouveauté Francaise*, 1921

Below
Selection of lingerie.
La Nouveauté Francaise, 1921

Right and opposite
A dressing gown with ruffling trimming
by Van Ultra. Underwood and
Underwood, c.1923

Selection of lingerie. Au Louvre
catalogue, 1925

Van Ultra

No. 112 Dressing Gown

Underwood & Underwood

LINGERIE POUR DAMES

26.753. **BONNET** de ménage zéphyr, fond blanc, dessins fantaisie. . . **3. »**

26.754. **BONNET** tulle garni entre-deux ondulé et dentelle. **6.90**

26.757. **CHEMISE JOUR** beau shirting, ornée feston et pois brodés main. **13. »**

26.758. **CHEMISE JOUR** madapolam souple, ornée dentelle de fil. **11.90**

26.756. **CHEMISE JOUR** beau madapolam, ornée feston. **11.50**

26.759. **CHEMISE JOUR** madapolam souple, ornée plis et feston main. **15. »**

26.755. **CHEMISE JOUR** madapolam ornée feston. **10.75**

26.760. **CHEMISE JOUR** beau madapolam, feston main, ornée point anglais. **17. »**

26.761. **KIMONO** nansouk orné broderie rose, mauve ou nattier. **12.90**

26.762. **CHEMISE NUIT** crépon blanc, ornée broderie rose, mauve ou nattier. **17.50**

26.763. **CHEMISE NUIT** madapolam, ornée plis et jours. **19. »**

26.768. **BONNET** tulle, motifs brodés et ruban. **9.90**

26.764. **CHEMISE NUIT** beau madapolam, ornée petits plis main et galon rouge. **19.50**

26.770. **BONNET** tulle, orné carrés filet et dentelle. **23. »**

26.765. **CHEMISIER** nansouk orné jours, en blanc, rose, mauve, citron. . . **23. »**

26.769. **BONNET** tulle, orné dentelle et ruban. **11.25**

26.766. **CHEMISE NUIT** beau shirting, empiècement brodé points main riches. **24. »**

26.767. **CHEMISIER** schappe, tout soie, orné jours. (En blanc, rose, mauve.) **69. »**

Chemise jour. **10.50** Culotte fermée. **10.50**
26.773. **PARURE** crépon blanc ou rose, ornée broderie et jours.

Chemise jour. **12.50** Culotte fermée. **12.50**
26.774. **PARURE** nansouk jours fils tirés et broderie main. (En rose ou citron.)

Culotte fermée. **9.90**
Chemise jour. **9.90**
26.772. **PARURE** nansouk, ornée entre-deux et bande brodée.

Chemise jour. **13. »** Culotte fermée. **13. »**
26.775. **PARURE** madapolam, feston et broderie main.

Chemise jour. **13.25** Culotte fermée. **13.25**
26.776. **PARURE** voile de coton broderie main et jours. (En rose, mauve, citron, ciel.)

Chemise jour. **9.25** Culotte fermée. **9.25**
26.771. **PARURE** nansouk, broderie main et jours.

Chemise jour. **14.50** Culotte fermée. **14.50**
26.777. **PARURE** beau nansouk, jours fils tirés et broderie main.

Chemise jour. **15. »** Culotte fermée. **15. »**
26.778. **PARURE** nansouk, forme Empire, feston et broderie main.

La lingerie du LOUVRE se recommande par sa qualité et le soin mis à son exécution.

Nº 703 · **COMBINAISON OPÉRA**
bord côtes en beau jersey soie, haut ajouré.
Se fait én : blanc, rose et mauve.
Prix : frs **135.** »

La culotte assortie, bord côtés.
Prix : frs **105.** »

Nº 705 · **CHEMISE CULOTTE**
forme enveloppe, en beau jersey fil mercerisé.
Se fait en : blanc, rose, mauve.
Prix : frs **45.** »
La culotte, bord côtes.
Prix : frs **39.** »
La combinaison Opéra, bord côtes
Prix : frs **55.** »

Nº 701 · **PARURE**

en toile fil et soie,
belle broderie et jours
main, belle dentelle
imitation.

Se fait en: rose, ivoire,
corail et mauve.

Prix : frs **165.** »

Nº 707 · **CHEMISE OPÉRA**
en beau jersey fil et soie.
Se fait en : blanc, rose et mauve
Prix : frs **49.** »

La culotte forme bouffant, avec
cocarde.. .. .. .. *frs* **55.** »
La culotte bord côtes. *frs* **49.** »
La combinaison Opéra bord
côtes. .. .. *frs* **55.** »

Above
Selection of lingerie by Maison Gerda.
Maison Gerda catalogue, c.1925

Other

Above
British Celanese Limited
advertisement for artificial silk
underwear, 1926

Pattern No. 40,183   Pattern No. 40,184   Pattern No. 40,185

Left
Satin boudoir jacket trimmed with
swansdown, nightdress and negligée
trimmed with marabou. *Fashions
for All*, 1927

Below
Selection of morning dresses, bed
jackets and housecoats. *Paris-Blouses*,
1920

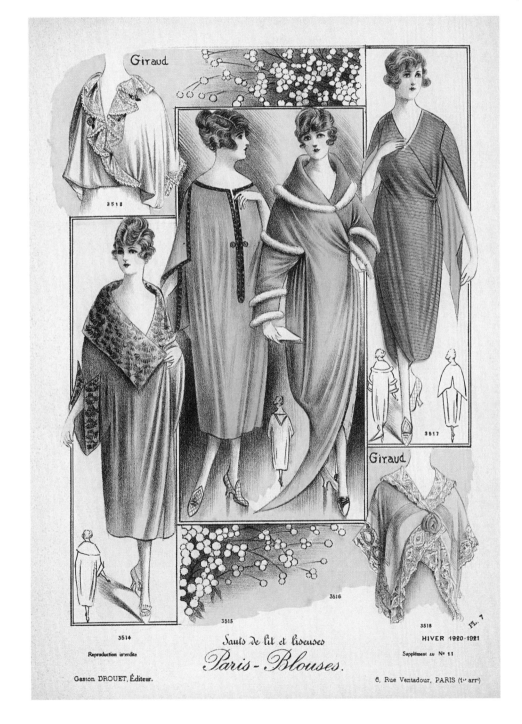

Other

Left
'A la ville voisine' (To the neighboring town), wedding dress by Jeanne Lanvin. Illustration by Pierre Brissaud. *Gazette du Bon Ton*, 1921

Above
Four elaborate wedding dresses with lace and net veils. *The Delineator*, 1922

Other

Right
A white wedding dress with a
cross-over bodice and gathered
side sash with a pearl headdress
and long veil, and a formal black
dress with lace flounce and cuffs.
La Femme Chic, c.1924

475

Other

Left
Actress Betty Bronson wearing a bridal gown, 1928. Betty Bronson starred in the silent movie *The Compassionate Marriage* which was retitled in Britain, *The Jazz Bride*.

Mode Pratique

DANS CE N°
Mariages Printaniers

Left
A lace wedding dress with a long
train and veil. *Mode Pratique*, 1926

Below
Cover of *L'Illustration des Modes*
showing bridal gown for a countryside
wedding by Beer, 1921

Left
Three models posing in a shop
window in London's West End, whilst
showing off the latest fashions in
swimwear and beach accessories,
c.1924

Right
Hollywood actress Shirley Mason
dressed in a satin one piece
swimming costume and matching
cap, accesorised with a large tassled
Spanish shawl with a batik print.
International newsreel photograph,
c.1924

Other

43-151

Above
A 'Leyland Bathing Cap'
advertisement, c.1927

Above
Photograph taken at a public
swimming pool in Sheffield,
England, c.1925

Other

Left and above
'Remords' (Remorse), hunting outfit. Illustration by Maurice Leroy. *Gazette du Bon Ton*, 1920

Advertisement for two ensembles for the beach or golfing by Jean Patou. *L'Illustration des Modes*, 1922

Other

488

Three women in tennis outfits.
Le Petit Echo de la Mode, 1921

Left and right
A skating suit with crêpe de Chine breeches, c.1924

A sport suit, possibly a skating or walking outfit, made up of breeches and a wool jumper dress with split details, c.1924

Right
A fashionable skiing ensemble
with knee socks, a buttoned cravat
fastening and matching fur hat and
scarf, c.1926

A 25069

Above
A model in a knitted sports coat
worked in a knit to resemble Astrakhan
fur in flaming orange worn with a
kash- coloured jersey skirt, c.1924

LA MODE-SPORT

Printemps-Été 1929

Sur une robe de crépella rouge vif, une veste de cuir
couleur ficelle. — En peau rouge, cette veste se b
tonnant jusqu'au col, est resserrée par une pe
ceinture. — Une vareuse en épais drap-cuir bla
de forme chic et nette. — Petite jaquette en d
Suède, garnie de poches à soufflets, col et rev
tailleur.

Above
Four sports skirt and leather jacket
ensembles for motoring and flying.
La Mode-Sport, c.1929

LA MODE·SPORT

Printemps-Eté 1929

Créations Jenny

Pour la plage, une jolie robe en kasha beige brodée de lignes de soie marron, orange, beige et blanc, effet de plastron lacé, col de gros-grain orangé. — Deux-pièces en jersey blanc tissé de rouge et bleu garni de bleu uni pour le pull-over, la jupe plissée est en crêpe de Chine bleu. — Cette jupe de marocain noir d'un effet très chic se porte avec un sweater en jersey vert et orangé réappliqué de marocain noir.

LA MODE·SPORT
Printemps-Été 1929

Planche 11

Sur une jupe en forme, en voile de laine rose Chine, un jumper à
impressions blanches et noires. — Un joli deux-pièces en lainage
uni canari pour la jupe et orné de cubes noirs, blancs et verts,
sur un côté du sweater. — Un ensemble de forme droite en
lainage angora blanc, imprimé sur le jumper de gros pois de faille dégradée verts cerclés de noir.
— D'une allure juvénile, ce deux-pièces jaune est en marocain de laine se colorant sur le pull-
over de rose cerné de noir et d'une fleur rose, verte et noire.

Modèles des Tissus d'Art
8, rue de Lévis

Left
Three beach outfits by Jenny. *La
Mode-Sport*, c.1929 – a beige Kasha
embroidered dress, a blue and white
jersey jumper with a red cravat detail
and paired with a blue crêpe de Chine
pleated skirt, and a back-pleated
dress worn with a green and orange
jersey jumper.

Above
Four sportswear outfits of dresses
and sweater-and-skirt ensembles.
La Mode-Sport, 1929

Other

LA MODE-SPORT

Printemps-Été 1929

Planche 5

Créations Jane Regny.

Un ensemble très réussi en lainage brun tabac, et
tricot beige pour le sweater, lequel s'ouvre à l'en-
colure ouverte en pointe, sur un plastron à petit
col rond en crêpe de Chine du ton, ceinture de cuir
fermée par une large boucle dorée. — D'un joli rouge brique ce trois-pièces comporte une jupe
en forme, une veste vague garnie de franges découpées à même le tissu, le pull-over en tricot blanc,
bleu et brique est ceinturé de cuir.

Above and right

Four sportswear ensembles by Jane
Regny. *La Mode-Sport*, 1929

Four tennis outfits in silk by Berthe
et Hermance. *La Mode Sport*, 1929

Printemps-Été 1929

Créations Berthe et Hermance

La Soie naturelle

Pour le tennis. — Rien de plus pratique et de plus joli que les tissus de soie naturelle. Souples et ne se déformant pas, ils résistent mieux que tous les autres, sous les coloris les plus délicats, aux ardeurs du soleil. — La première de ces robes est en belle toile de soie blanche; la seconde en shantung rose, ornée de piqûres de soie bleu de cobalt; la troisième, élargie de plis sur les côtés, est en crêpe de Chine blanc, ceinturée de Suède bleu; la quatrième, un charmant deux-pièces en soie schappe coupée de bandes de crêpe rouge et bleu. — Les légers tissus de soie naturelle, qui peuvent être lavés indéfiniment, sont les plus pratiques pour les sports et la campagne.

BIOGRAPHIES

Beer
Parisian Couture House
1905 – 1929

The German designer Gustav Beer moved to Paris in 1905 to found Maison Beer, which specialised in conservative feminine daywear and evening wear and was particularly known for its lingerie collections. Gustav Beer was the first designer to open on the Place Vendôme. He would visit big luxurious hotels to sell his collections to tourists and as his popularity grew he opened couture salons in Nizza, Italy and in Monte Carlo. In 1931 the fashion house merged with Agnes-Drecoll, although Beer dresses continued to be made until 1953. Located at 7 Place Vendôme, Paris.

Alice Bernard
Parisian Couture House
c.1916 – c.1926

Little is known about the Maison of Alice Bernard although its designs featured in several publications throughout the first half of the 1920s. A reference appears in the French press when in 1923 the fashion house's seamstresses went on strike over pay. Located at 40 Rue Francois, Paris.

Bernard et Cie
Parisian Couture House
Active 1920s and 1930s

Bernard et Cie was originally founded as a tailoring company in 1905 by M. Bernard in partnership with M. Jourda and M. Hirsch. The firm produced tailor-made costumes, afternoon dresses, evening gowns, coats and furs. Their garments were notable for their elegant slender silhouettes and elaborate detailing. In 1915, the New York Times stated, "Bernard, who is always an American favorite, has a collection of more than 100 modes". Certainly the famous American department store, Bonwit Teller carried many Bernard et Cie models, with prices as high as $550. The firm's heyday was during the 1910s and 1920s, however, it continued operating until the mid-1930s. Located 33 Avenue de l'Opera, Paris.

Jane Blanchot
Parisian Millinery Company
c.1921 – c.1949

Jane Blanchot was a sculptoress and continued to devote herself to her vocation, whilst also pursuing a career as milliner, which began in 1910 with the opening of an atelier in Paris. Until the 1960s, she designed hats, exploring sculptural forms and innovative structures. Her passion for sculpture also found an outlet in her creation of jewelry.

After the war, as honorary President of the Chambre Syndicale de la Couture, she struggled to safeguard artisan perfectionism within the fashion profession. Located at 11 Faubourg St-Honore, Paris.

Doeuillet
Parisian Couture House
1900 – 1939

Georges Doeuillet was born in France in 1875. He started out as a silk merchant, and later trained with the Soeurs Callots as their business manager. He subsequently established his own eponymous fashion house in 1900, and the same year exhibited at the Paris Exhibition. He became the first designer to make *robe-de-styles*, what we now call cocktail dress. The house was best known for its detailed dresses and elaborate designs, and for parading live mannequins at the beginning of each season's showings. In 1915, he included in his collection, a black velvet and taffeta dress with the newly popular tiered handkerchief hem, and two years later introduced the barrel-line silhouette. In 1919, one of his gowns was a white satin brocade chemise with the new straight look and short skirt, which anticipated the look of the 20s. In 1926, he was fashionable up-to-date with his very short-skirted black satin dress, brocaded with flowers, with an uneven butterfly hem. Doeuillet had an exclusivity contract with *Gazette du Bon Ton* to promote his fashions. He took over from Doucet when the former died in 1929 and continued designing for both houses for nearly another decade. The house closed in 1937. Located at 24 Place Vendôme, Paris.

Drecoll
Viennese and Parisian Couture House
1900/02 – 1929

A Belgian Baron, Christophe von Drecoll originally founded the House of Drecoll in Vienna in 1896. The house designed Belle Époque fashions for the Imperial family of Austria. In 1902 the Couture house Drecoll opened in Paris and was run by Monsieur and Madame Besancon de Wagner who had bought the business and the right to the name. In 1929 their daughter-in-law, the designer Maggie Rouff took over the business. In 1931 the firm merged again this time with Maison Agnes. Maison Agnes-Drecoll eventually closed in 1963. The maison was known for two distinct styles. In the Belle Époque period Drecoll specialised in fussy and luxuriously trimmed promenade gowns, tea gowns and evening dresses with boned bodices and full skirts. In the 1920's, however, the house was known for short, simple and elegant dresses. Located 130 Avenues des Champs-Elysées and 4, Place de l'Opéra, and later at 24 Place Vendôme, Paris.

Groult
Parisian Couture House
1912 – early 1960s

The sister of Paul Poiret, Pauline Marie Poiret (1887–1966) initially trained at her brother's house before setting up her own maison as Nicole Groult. She was married to the French decorator and furniture designer, André Groult (1884 – 1966) hence the house name. She was known for two styles in particular – simple black dresses with coloured detailing and colourful tea dresses. Located at 29 Rue d'Anjou, Pairs.

Heim
Parisian Haute Couture House
1899 – 1967

Maison Heim
1930 – 1969

Jacques Heim started his career as the manager of Isadore and Jeanne Heim's fur fashion house. Around 1925 he set up a couture department for coats, suits, and gowns and in 1930 he opened his own couture house. Heim never allied himself to a particular look or style, which is the main reason why he is not remembered as a fashion innovator. Instead his fashions moved easily with the times, which was the key to the house's longevity. Heim was president of the Chambre Syndicale de la Couture Parisienne from 1958 to 1962. Located at 48 Rue Laffitte, Paris.

Jenny
Parisian Couture House
1908 – 1938

The House of Jenny was known for its simple and comfortable sports fashions and leisurewear. In 1927 Jenny designed the wardrobe for Miss France. In 1938, Jeanne Bernard merged her firm with the house of Lucile Paray. It finally closed in 1940 when the Germans occupied Paris. Madame Bernard died in 1961 at the age of 89. Located at 70 Avenue des Champs-Elysées, Paris.

Jeanne Lanvin
Parisian Couturier
1867 – 1946

Maison Lanvin
1909 – present

Jeanne Lanvin trained as a milliner at Madame Félix and as dressmaker at Talbot. She later became a member of the Syndicat de la Couture in 1909. Lanvin started making children's clothes after being asked for copies of the dresses she had made for her daughter. Soon she was also dressing their mothers and coordinated mother and daughter outfits became a mainstay of her work. Lanvin was famed for her exquisite *robes de style* – dresses inspired by historic styles characterised by full skirts sometimes supported with petticoats or panniers. In the 1920s Lanvin opened shops devoted to home interiors and lingerie. Lanvin also opened a menswear boutique in 1926 and was responsible for the decoration of the Pavilion d'Elegance at the 1925 Exposition Internationale des Arts Décoratifs et Industriels Modernes. After her death the House of Lanvin was passed down to her daughter Marguerite di Pietro and is still in operation today having changed hands several times. Located at 22 Rue du Faubourg Saint-Honoré, Paris.

Margaine-Lacroix
Parisian Couture Designer
c.1889 – c.1929

Jeanne Margaine-Lacroix rose to fame during the Belle Époque period. Margaine-Lacroix won a gold medal for corsetry at the 1899 Paris exhibition. She is credited with creating the Sheath dress and slashed skirts (1912) and the Sylphide corset and sinuously curved Sylphide dress. In 1908, three models wearing her tight empire style gowns were arrested at the Longchamp racecourse for their own safety as their garments were considered too shocking (it is suggested they were so tight they split at the sides when the models bent down). During World War I she collaborated with artist Albert Marque and commissioned him to create a hundred fashion dolls, which she clothed in French historic outfits and regional costumes. Louis Sue of Sue & Mare designed the shop's interior. Located at 19 Boulevard Haussman and later found at 29 Avenue du Marigny.

Martial et Armand
Parisian Couture House
Active 1920s – 1940s

There are references to Martial et Armand of Paris as far back as 1830 but it is unclear what the firm was producing at this point or if this was indeed the same firm as the couture house. The house is mentioned often in 1920s fashion magazines as specialising in couture dresses, furs and lingerie. The house launched its own perfume around 1924, while the designer Pauline Trigere trained at the house in the 1930s. Located at 10 Place Vendome and 13 Rue de la Paix, Paris.

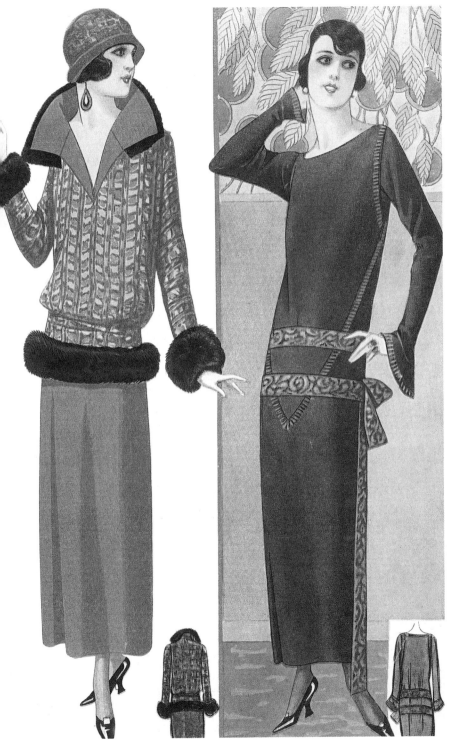

Left
Five designs for the first days of spring
– a black dress by Welly Soeurs, a
red dress by Jean Patou, a black coat
by Heim, a fur trimmed jumper suit by
Jean Paton and a brown crepe dress
with a patterned sash. *Le Femme
Chic*, c.1925

BIOGRAPHIES

Patou
Parisian Couture House
1919 – present

Jean Patou (1880 – 1936) opened the small dressmaking shop called Maison Parry in 1912. After serving in World War I he returned to Paris and reopened his business under his own name. Patou was best known for his sportswear and sports fashions. He dressed tennis legend Suzanne Lenglen both on and off the court. In 1925 he opened a Parisian boutique named Le Coin des Sports (The Sports Corner), a shop with a series of rooms each devoted to a different sport. Outfits and accessories for aviation, riding, swimming, tennis, golf and several others were stocked and met with great success. Patou capitalised on the leisure industry and opened salons in the upmarket resorts of Deauville and Biarritz selling his trademark casual chic fashions. He was the first designer to embellish his sweaters and sportswear with his initials and he launched the first designer sun lotion 'Huile de Caldée' in 1928. The house has stopped producing fashion collections but remains open as a perfume house Located at 7 Rue Saint-Florentin, Paris.

Élise Poret
Parisian Couturier
Active 1910s – 1920s

Little is known about the Parisian fashion designer, Élise Poret other than she created elegant Belle Époque dresses during the 1910s. She also designed lingerie and nightwear. During the 1920s she also designed Grecian-inspired ensembles. Located at 20 Rue des Capucines, Paris.

Paul Poiret
Parisian Haute Couturier
1879 – 1944

Maison Poiret
1903 – 1929

Poiret began his design career by selling sketches to Madeleine Cheruit. In 1896 he was hired by the fashion designer Jacques Doucet, and later moved to the House of Worth in 1901. He established his own fashion house in 1903, and made his name with the kimono coat. Mostly remembered for his straight silhouettes, his hobble skirt, harem pantaloons, lampshade tunics and for liberating women from the s-bend corset and petticoats. He equally had a shrewd instinct for marketing and branding, promoting the total designer lifestyle and established the perfume company, Rosine and the interior decorating company, Atelier Martine. His influence on modern fashion both in terms of design and business achievements is formidable. He was one of the first courtiers to introduce perfume into his product line. By 1920s, however, his luxurious Oriental fashions were being supplanted by more functional and rational styles. Poiret took part in the "Exposition Internationale des Arts Décoratifs et Industriels Modernes" of 1925, where he showed his creations in barges along the River Seine, however, such an expensive display appears to have been a financial disaster and the house was eventually forced to close in 1929. Located at 1 Rond-Point des Champs-Elysées, Paris.

Premet
Parisian Couture House
1911 – 1931

Madame Charlotte, often referred to as the most beautiful woman in Paris and easily recognisable with her pale mauve hair, succeeded Mme. Lefranc as head-designer for Maison Premet in 1918. The house is best known for its 1923 La Garçonne model, a simple black dress with white collar and cuffs. Over a million copies of the dress are said to have sold in the USA alone. Premet is credited with introducing the 1920s 'gamine look' by raising hemlines, pioneering low cut backs and the use of light and floaty materials. In 1923 Germaine Krebs, (later known as Alix and then Madame Grès) trained with the house for several months. In 1928 Premet collaborated with watchmakers Elgin to produce an exclusive design for the American market. Located at 8 Place Vendôme, Paris.

Redfern
Parisian & London
Couture House
est. 1891 – 1940

Charles Poynter Redfern (1850 – 1929) was the son of English designer John Redfern, who had been the dressmaker to Queen Victoria and various members of the British aristocracy. In 1881 Charles Poynter Redfern established his own fashion house in Paris, which became known for his elegant blue ladies' suits as well as for the elaborate costumes that he created for actress Sarah Bernhardt. He also employed extremely attractive sales assistants to promote his fashions and they became known as the "Redferns Bunnies". His tailoring section was directed to the market generated by the famous Cowes week held every August. While his son, Ernest, managed the London branch of the business, Redfern himself looked after the company's Paris branch. Other branches were also opened in Cowes, London, Edinburgh, Manchester, Paris, Nice, Aix-les-Bains, Cannes, New York, Chicago and Newport, Rhode Island. In 1892, John

Redfern & Sons was formally incorporated and so began its development from the most successful ladies' tailoring business to an international couture enterprise equal of Worth. The company's aggressive advertising in the most important fashion journals in Britain and the cultivation of royal patrons made a 'Redfern' the desired dress of women around the world. By 1885, Maison Redfern was producing yachting, riding, and travelling suits and was not only the officially appointed dressmaker to Queen Victoria, but also counted the Empress of Russia as another client. In 1916 Redfern designed the first women's uniform for the Red Cross. In 1911 he declared that "the cultured American lady is the best-dressed lady in the world" and he continued to create elegant if somewhat somber fashions during the 1920s. The Redfern fashion houses closed in 1932, briefly reopened in 1936, and closed again in 1940. Located 242 Rue de Rivoli, Paris & 27, Old Bond Street, London.

Jane Regny
Parisian Couture House
Active 1920s & 1930s

A keen golfer and tennis player, Jane Regny was sports editor of the Annuaire des Golfs and specialised in sports fashions. During the 1920s and 1930s, she was as well known and successful as Chanel and Patou for her comfortable and stylish creations. Located at 11 Rue de la Boetie, Paris.

Reville
London Couture House
1906 – 1949

Mr William Wallace Terry Reville and Miss Rossiter, who had both previously worked as buyers for Jay's department store, founded Reville in 1906. During its existence the company operated under several names and was the court dressmaker to Queen Mary, designing her coronation robe in 1911. William Wallace Terry Reville worked as the house's designer, while Rossiter was in charge of running the business. It gained a royal warrant in 1910, which ensured it subsequently became patronised by the leading members of London society. By the 1920s Reville's garments seemed rather outdated, as they did not seamlessly adapt to the newer modern styles like some of their competitors, and the firm eventually merged with the London branch of Worth during the late 1930s. Located at 15 – 17 Hanover Square, London.

Suzanne Talbot
Parisian Modiste and Couture Milliner
c.1914 – c.1947

Suzanne Talbot's real name was Madame Mathieu Levy and she is considered one of the most important modistes of the 20th century. Lanvin was apprenticed with Talbot and she was an early patron of Eileen Gray and commissioned her to design her stylish apartment in Rue de Lota, Paris in 1919. Located at 10 Rue Royale, Paris.

Welly Soeurs
Parisian Couture House
Active 1920s – 1930s

Specialising in couture clothes and sportswear, the Welly Soeurs fashion house was founded by Cécile Welly and her sister. The former was also responsible for founding the children's couture house, Mignapouf. Located at 21 Faubourg Saint Honore, Paris.

Worth
Parisian Couture House
1858 – 1956

Charles Frederick Worth (1825 – 1895) established the first haute couture house in Paris in 1858, offering bespoke garments chosen by clients from a seasonal portfolio. Maison Worth had the royal patronage of Empress Eugénie and Princess Pauline von Metternich. The fashion house was known for its exquisite designs and execution. It was also one of the first couture houses to extend its name to luxury perfume in 1924. After Worth's death, his sons Gaston-Lucien and Jean-Phillipe took over the business which merged with Paquin only two years short of its centenary in 1956. Located at 7 Rue de la Paix, Paris.

Below
Illustration of various winter outfits.
La Mode, 1920

Luoy.

4076

INDEX

BIBLIOGRAPHY

1920s Fashions from B.Altman and Company, Dover Publications, 1999

Baudot, F., *A Century of Fashion*, Thames & Hudson, 1999

Blackman, C., *20th Century Fashion: The 20s and 30s Flappers and Vamps*, Heinemann Library

Blum, S. *Everyday Fashions of the 20's* (Dover Books on Costume), Dover Publications, 1999

Chadwick, W., *The Modern Woman Revisited: Paris between the Wars*, Rutgers University Press, 2003

Chahine, N., *Beauty: The 20th Century*, Universe, 2000

Chenoune, F., *Hidden Femininity: 20th Century Lingerie*, Assouline, 1999

Entwistle, J., *The Fashioned Body: Fashion, Dress and Modern Social Theory*, Polity Press, 2000

Gaines, J. & Herzog, C., *Fabrications: Costume and the Female Body*, Routledge, 1990

Herald, J., *Fashions of a Decade: 1920s*, Facts of File Inc., 2006

Hollander, A., *Seeing Through Clothes*, University of California Press, 1993

Horwood, C., *Keeping Up Appearances: Fashion and Class Between the Wars*, The History Press, 2011

Kirke, B., *Madeleine Vionnet*, Chronicle Books, 1998

Langley, S. & Dowling, J., *Roaring '20s Fashions: Deco*, Schiffer Publishing, 2005

Lehmann, U., *Tigersprung : Fashion in Modernity*, MIT Press, 2000

Lehnert, G., *A History of Fashion in the 20th Century*, Konemann, 2000

Mackrell, A., *Coco Chanel*, Holmes & Meier, 1992

Martin, R., *Cubism and Fashion*, Metropolitan Museum of Art, 1998

Martin, R. & Koda, H., *Orientalism: Visions of the East in Western Dress*, Metropolitan Museum of Art, 1994

Mendes, V. & de la Haye, A., *20th Century Fashion*, Thames & Hudson, 1999

Muller, F., *Art & Fashion*, Thames & Hudson, 2000

Pattison, A & Cawthorne, N., *A Century of Shoes: Icons of Style in the Twentieth Century*, Chartwell Books, 1997

Rasche, A., *STYL: The Early 1920s German Fashion Magazine: Das Modejournal der frühen 1920er Jahre*, Arnoldsche, 2009

Richards, M., *Chanel: Key Collections*, Hamlyn, 2000

Steele, V., *Paris Fashion: A Cultural History*, Berg, 1988

Stewart, M., *Dressing Modern Frenchwomen: Marketing Haute Couture, 1919-1939*, The John Hopkins University Press, 2008

Vassiliev, A., *Beauty in Exile: the Artists, Models and Nobility who fled the Russian Revolution and influenced the World of Fashion*, Abrams, 2000

Watson, L., *"Vogue" Twentieth Century Fashion: 100 Years of Style by Decade and Designer*, Carlton, 1999

Wigley, M., White Walls, *Designer Dresses: the Fashioning of Modern Architecture*, MIT Press, 1995

Wilson, E. & Taylor, L., *Through the Looking Glass: a History of Dress from 1860 to the Present Day*, BBC Books, 1989

Wilson, E., *Adorned in Dreams: Fashion and Modernity*, Virago, 1987

Wollen, P., *Addressing the Century: 100 years of Art and Fashion*, Hayward Gallery Publishing, 1998

ACKNOWLEDGEMENTS & CREDITS

This project has been a wonderful learning experience as well as a fascinating trip into the world of fashion history. Firstly I would like to offer my immense gratitude to Emmanuelle Dirix for her good-natured perseverance and infectious passion, as well as for her wonderful introduction and skillful captioning. I would also like to thank my daughter, Clementine for her insightful help with picture sourcing and Guy Jackson for his wonderful work on the graphic design side of things, especially his tireless enthusiasm for getting the layout absolutely right. Thanks must also go to Zöe Fawcett for her wonderful help with the production of this title and to Rosanna Negrotti for her painstaking copy-editing. And lastly, an acknowledgement of gratitude to Isabel Wilkinson and her forensic checking of captions. A big thank you to everyone!

We regret that in some cases it has not been possible to trace the original copyright holders of early publicity photographs or from earlier publications. We have, however, endeavoured to respect the right of third parties and if any such rights have been overlooked in individual cases, the mistake will be correspondingly amended where possible.

The all images used in this publication were sourced from the Fiell Archive, London, with the exception of:

Emmanuelle Dirix: Breakspread, 20, 414, 415, 480, 481

TopFoto (TopFoto.co.uk): 200–201

ABOUT THE AUTHORS

Charlotte Fiell

Charlotte Fiell is a leading authority on the history, theory and criticism of design and has written over 60 books on the subject. She initially trained at the British Institute in Florence, before studying at Camberwell College of Arts (UAL), London, from which she received a BA(Hons) in the History of Drawing and Printmaking with Material Science. She later trained at Sotheby's Institute of Art in London. In the late 1980s she opened with her husband, Peter, a pioneering design gallery in London's King's Road and through this acquired a rare hands-on knowledge of modern design. In 1991, the Fiells' first book *Modern Furniture Classics since 1945* was published to widespread acclaim. Since then, the Fiells have concentrated on communicating design more widely through authorship, curation, and teaching. Her most recent titles include: *100 Ideas that Changed Design*, *Women in Design: From Aino Aalto to Eva Zeisel* and *Ultimate Collector Cars*.

Introduction by Emmanuelle Dirix

Emmanuelle Dirix is a highly regarded fashion historian and curator. She lectures on Critical and Historical studies at Winchester School of Art, Central Saint Martins, the Royal College of Art and the Antwerp Fashion Academy. She regularly contributes to exhibition catalogues and academic volumes. Projects include the exhibition and book *Unravel: Knitwear in Fashion*, *1920s Fashion: The Definitive Sourcebook* and *1930s Fashion: The Definitive Sourcebook*.